Slater's Crimson China
Vivian Ward

ROSA ANTIPODES

The Rose Gardens, Christchurch, N.Z.
J.C. Smith, Photo, Wellington N.Z. Prot. CN03

ROSA ANTIPODES

The history of roses in New Zealand

Keith Stewart

David Bateman

Acknowledgements

This work would never have been started, or finally appeared, had it not been for the support of Ian Grant, a rare writers' friend who cares for things done, and the people who do them.

Thanks also to Ann Clifford and Tracey Borgfeldt who knew better than I when I got things wrong, but was too stubborn to see, and also for Tracey's even temper during the fraught months of tracking down illustrations.

To Vivian Ward, and Dennis Watkins who recommended her. Vivian's paintings for the book, and her wonderful mezzotints, have captured an essential rose image so often neglected by artists in their attempts to reproduce years of chocolate boxes and calendars. Alan Sinclair and Theo Verryt at Roseneath, Toni Sylvester from her own gorgeous garden, and the staff at the Parnell Rose Gardens, who were generous in their help with roses for the paintings.

Donald Kerr of the Rare Books Room at the Auckland Central City Library was an outstanding supporter throughout the research period, and he helped untangle many convoluted paths. The Auckland Central City Library and the Alexander Turnbull Library both proved to be superb research facilities, with the photographic, print, cartoon, and ephemera archives at the Turnbull being particularly helpful at all stages. Thanks also to Aiden Challis who pointed me in the right direction at the very beginning.

A special thanks also to the families of some of our great rosarians who shared their special whakapapa with me. To Alan and Mary Mason; June and Laurie Bell, and Bronwyn Cornish of Bell Roses; and Frank Schuurman. Eric Bullen, the last of the famous Lippiatt line, was wonderful in his recollections and priceless memorabilia, material that proved to be a critical link with 'The Boss', W. E. Lippiatt.

Sam McGredy was also a very important figure in making this book, not just because of the help he provided, but for the contribution he has made to the history of roses here, for his international perspective, his fabulous roses, and his marvellous enthusiasm.

Published in 1994 by David Bateman Ltd, "Golden Heights", 32–34 View Road, Glenfield, Auckland, New Zealand

Copyright © Keith Stewart, 1994
Copyright © David Bateman Ltd, 1994

ISBN 1 86953 163 9

Front cover: Aotearoa
Back cover: The Rose Garden, Botanic Gardens, Christchurch

Paintings and mezzo-tints by Vivian Ward
Designed by Errol McLeary
Typeset by Jazz Graphics
Printed in Hong Kong by Colorcraft

Contents

Dedication

Roses are for love; this work is for Julie.

Introduction

$\mathbf{A}$s the sailing ship *Ann* scuttled across a blustery Bay of Biscay in the autumn of 1809, en route to New South Wales with a fresh contingent of transportees for the penal colony, two strangers seeking the wind and space of her decks had a chance meeting that began the process of forming a nation of the people and islands of New Zealand. One, in the conservative dress of a clergyman, was principal chaplain of New South Wales, and he was drawn by the obvious distress of the other, who was huddled, sick and cold, in the vessel's fo'c's'le, wearing only a ragged greatcoat to keep out the wind.

The chaplain was the Reverend Samuel Marsden, returning after consultation with his superiors on matters that included Marsden's plans to establish a church settlement in New Zealand in advance of a missionary incursion. The other man aroused Marsden's interest because he was a New Zealander, obviously in need of friendship and medical attention, and, judging by his tattoos, a man of importance amongst his own people. The missionary in Marsden saw this young New Zealander as God's providence, an opportunity to further his evangelical designs.

Under the greatcoat was Ruatara, an intelligent and perceptive Ngapuhi rangatira who had worked on whaling and sealing ships in order to find out more about the Pakeha world. He had been deceived and abused by sea captains, and deserted, unpaid and virtually naked, in London at the conclusion of his last voyage. His attempts to meet the King of England had been ridiculed, and he had every reason to mistrust and despise Pakeha, but his mind told him that there was something to

9

be gained for his people from Pakeha technology, particularly from their gardening and agriculture. Ruatara was a visionary of immense significance, and he saw that the friendship that Marsden offered him could be as valuable to his own plans as Marsden thought it was to his.

Marsden's kindness restored Ruatara's health enough for him to work his passage back to Sydney, where he stayed with Marsden on his extensive farm at Parramatta for ten months, learning all he could of the Pakeha ways of horticulture and agriculture. When he returned to his hapu in the Bay of Islands, he had with him the material and plans for New Zealand's first adventure in exporting food, and he left Marsden with a promise that he could start his advance settlement on land under Ruatara's protection. When Ruatara later travelled back to Sydney with his uncle Hongi Hika to help Marsden execute his missionary dream, on his return journey he brought back the first roses to be planted in New Zealand.

It is not unusual for roses to be part of such profound history, for roses have a spiritual symbolism that is far deeper than we imagine and a mysterious luck that keeps them at the centre of things. Perhaps it was the spiritual draw of the first New Zealand roses' crimson blooms that attracted Ruatara's attention, but it was a spiritualism that owed nothing to thousands of years of European belief. Was Ruatara's attraction a reflection of the same appeal roses had when they were first adopted as religious images, or was it simply luck?

Whatever it was, roses are not simple flowers, and their place in New Zealand has not been just the result of roses' hungry vigour in such a fertile land. Roses are pretty, very pretty, but they stand for sex and love, power and death, the rhythm of our lives, and while we may be located far in the Pacific blue, our spiritual roots stretch across the world to the darkest pagan rituals that also kept these rhythms and painted them with roses.

Whenever roses' elevated place in our minds has been challenged, the rose mystery has brought them forward again with another facet to their character, a new image for the new time. The conquering Greeks took it from Persia, and the Romans from the Greeks. Christianity rejected then embraced the rose; the Italian Renaissance elevated it in its art; science rediscovered it; and just as Europe was reordering itself, with Napoleon's bullying, his empress, Josephine, was championing roses as never before.

'Code Napoleon' transformed the administration of Western Europe, and Josephine's passion elevated roses to a popularity they had not enjoyed since Roman times. A population explosion came with the peace that ended Napoleon's wars, and its force scattered Europeans and their culture across the world, liberally sprinkling burgeoning colonies with roses' new popularity. New Zealand was a part of this phenomenon from its very beginning. Nurtured by their own symbolic references to the old European world and an idyllic new society yet to be made, roses thrived in this fertile place, their virility allowing them to adopt a range of new roles while consolidating the old.

Roses flourish here in every way, and when the mystery brought Sam McGredy to New Zealand 170 years after Ruatara's return, it was the final step in a process that has established New Zealand as one of the great rose centres of the world, a step that has given roses another home. Here it is now wild and tamed, traditional and modern, amateur and commercial. Here its image, its history, and its culture thrive. Here it is celebrated in private and in public with almost unmatched enthusiasm.

Not that New Zealand is alone in this celebration, for the culture of internationalism that now spans our increasingly global community maintains the rose in its privileged position, either as a commercial tool, attached by brand and advertising to diverse merchandise, or as a mark of prestige. We are part of this whole, branded world of commerce and international images, and roses, once invited guests, are no longer foreigners but part of a New Zealand that has grown into that world.

The history of roses here is a history of all of us, and their evolution from the time of Ruatara's invitation to Sam McGredy's export of New Zealand-raised pedigrees is very much the evolution of a new country and a new people.

1 The rose mystery

Footfalls echo in the memory
Down the passage we did not take
Towards the door we never opened
Into the rose garden.

Burnt Norton, *T. S. Eliot*

Aotearoa is a handsome symbol of the young country whose name it carries. Young, big and beautiful, like some blushing colonial girl grown strong on healthy air, it is a rose so bold, so fragrant, so pink, that it is at once a caricature of the English rose-beauty that lives in our minds and a symbol of an old culture reborn. A link with the past and a hope for the future, its striking fertility epitomises the generations of roses which have stood for the universal woman, who as the great goddess is mother of the world for so many religions. Suitably brazen for the time, Aotearoa is a modern version of the rose mystery; a mystery with New Zealand flavours, but one that remains alive with a million memories of generations past — subtle and secret memories held by intimate histories of the heart as well as by institutionalised culture.

Symbolism is not always so forthright as Aotearoa, and roses are both too subtle in their imagery to be taken seriously by most people and so obvious that we often fail to notice how influential some of their ancient references are. Mythology and symbolism are the stuff of fairy tales in this bright, modern world informed by science rather than religion, but it is surprising how quickly we recognise the signposts that some call superstition, and how frequently we use them. The gift of a dozen roses still speaks of love as clearly as it ever did, or of lust, and the roses around us in our gardens and our other art forms are messages left by millions of years of passion, messages with which we guide ourselves through the dramas of life, and if we care to, take many small pleasures from on the way.

Sex is what roses speak of most frequently, and most loudly, or, more precisely, female sexuality and the male urge to indulge in it, breathe it, touch it. Even in its simplest form, as a single, five-petalled bloom from one of the ancient species, the rose symbolises female sex, and there has never been anything subtle about this carnal association. It is so direct, so urgent, that ever since humans have been tampering with roses they have shaped them more and more into gently turned floral replicas of the vulva, slowly unfurling from bud to open flower.

This sculptural homage to femininity is obvious in the extravagant curl of Aotearoa's pink petals, but no less so in tender garden roses as old as the classic Cuisse de Nymphe (Nymph's Thigh). Perhaps the horticultural artists who crafted such flowers took the idea of art copying nature to its logical conclusion, this time with the help of Mother Nature. If so, the great goddess maintains a strong presence in our gardens and our minds whether we acknowledge it or not. Maybe this presence is just coincidence, but the line of rose breeding that has evolved into such an explicit symbol as Aotearoa is so long it suggests otherwise.

Whatever the ancient catalyst behind the cultivation and hybridising of roses, they have remained extremely evocative, especially when shape is combined with the soft touch of petals, their traditional pale hues, frequently tinted with red to the colour of flesh and beyond, and a luxurious fragrance that still sets them apart from other flowers. It really is no wonder that roses are the most well-worked allegory for womanly beauty in every Western language, and more than a few from the East as well.

We even retain some of the festivals associated with fertility rites for the venerable goddess. Mothers' Day is the most obvious, a celebra-

Lusty rose allegories are as relevant, and obvious, in late twentieth-century New Zealand as they were in Renaissance Florence.

"Eloise", Fiona Pardington

tion of fecund woman that has been held in May through 2000 years of Christianity back to ancient Rome, and probably even further back, into the most primitive tribal religions. For the Romans, this day of honouring motherhood was a rose festival tribute to Flora, the great goddess in her bountiful guise as ruler over fruit trees, vineyards and flowers. Along the balmy fringes of the Mediterranean, that Maytime celebration would have been awash with roses in their first flush, and statues of the goddess would have been adorned with cascades of garlands and bouquets. Mothers, too, were honoured as living representatives of Flora, and given gifts of roses much they still are by their children each Mothers' Day. Husbands, daughters and sons throughout the Western world, rose bouquets firmly in hand, now pay homage to the gift of life that women grant in a way that remains entirely appropriate after thousands of years. Their floral tributes also serve as reminders that roses are not just pretty flowers, that their mystery continues to hold our minds in ways we hardly ever recognise.

Mothers are also lovers; or at least they once were. The great goddess, too, puts on other masks and takes herself to play with men on a field of love strewn with roses. Aphrodite, Venus, call her what you will, she is a wanton in pursuit of pleasure without concern for morals — the spirit of licentiousness, goddess of love, inventor of recreational sex. Her rose is no gift of honour, but an invitation to bed, a temptation and celebration of youth. This is the love of lust, albeit with consequences of procreation and subsequent domesticity; but in the heat of Aphrodite's bed there are no consequences, just satisfaction. These roses are the deep red roses of passion. According to Botticelli, Aphrodite was born of sea foam amidst a storm of roses, and roses are her flower and Venus' after her. To these ancient ladies you could add every mistress and bimbo from the courts of France to Hollywood. Every woman whose fame has been her sexual prowess, whose beauty has been sexual, whose availability has been spoken of in roses. A continuous goddess through ages of lust, with a rose clenched between her teeth, set at the table or strewn on the floor.

It is always roses, even to the bed of roses that remains a universal dream of bliss. That famous bed was written into our literary tradition by the great English poet Spenser. He set roses about his Elizabethan beauty, the Faerie Queene, in lines that lavished such sensuality they sent a carnal shiver down generations of readers, and transferred from old traditions of Roman indulgence a standard for rose allegory rich with sexual innuendo.

> *Upon a bed of Roses she was layd,*
> *As faint through heat, or dight to pleasant sin,*
> *And was arayd, or rather disarayd,*
> *All in a vele of silke and silver thin,*
> *That hid no whit her alabaster skin.*

The Faerie Queene Book II, Canto xii

Such steam imitates Aphrodite, as Spenser fully intended, and acts as a companion to the many carnal urges that bubble beneath the bland surface of social order. But Aphrodite did not play alone, and to ancient

Greeks the god of this primaeval pot was the horned and rampant Dionysus, called Bacchus by the Romans. An amoral deity, his floral symbol was also the rose, in part because sexual lust crossed his boundaries, but also because the rose plant is a living paradox, thorns as well as blossom, an allegory for the pain that runs with pleasure in an uncivilised world.

This disturbing aspect of rose symbolism has faded with time, and even Dionysus himself is recollected today as the god of parties and wine rather than the spirit who drove women followers to tear limbs from babies and fornicate with goats. The old god played for keeps, his realm of abandonment lacking any trace of moderation, so it is not surprising that his cult should have been tamed by civilised memory and the volatile urges of his territory denied any religious legitimacy.

But Dionysus serves to remind us of the very fundamental character of the rose mystery, its roots worked deep into the most profound aspects of life. Indeed, the rose mystery is itself an allegory for life's mysterious cycle and as such addresses itself to death as much as it does to love and life. There are roses on graves, carved into headstones and printed on cards of sympathy, much as they are on wedding invitations. Roses and death — their partnership goes as far back as our cultural memory, as far back as love and roses, as far as wine and roses, effectively forever.

So the rose we know is not so much a garden plant as a spiritual flower that captures in its symbolism the essentials of human life: the truth of the circular dynamic of sex, birth, life and death. Perhaps it is this aspect of the rose, the spiritual rose that stands behind garden roses, that has made it such a consummate colonist; one whose imagery slips as easily into the lines of a Maori poet as it did into Spenser's verse, or can be used with equal effect to epitomise the beauty of Cantonese, Indian or Egyptian women. To cover such a range the rose must be quick, must move its allegiance from one stage to the next with the smoothness of a wheel; and it does.

Soon after roses have invited us to bed they appear in bridal bouquets, a subtle sign of the change from maidenhood to impending motherhood. The red rose of passion has fast become the pink rose of beauty ripening, growing life. The bridal bouquet is traditionally a circlet, roses in a ring, the beginning of another life cycle; 'Ring a ring a roses,' as the old nursery rhyme goes. This was the rose that Shakespeare laid out for us so carefully. 'From fairest creatures we desire increase, That thereby beauty's rose might never die,' he wrote, showing the promise of everlasting beauty that the cycle offers. Quite simply he made in words the circlet of the rose mystery, showing how regenerating life denies death, how beauty holds its own eternity.

The simplicity of the rose/life mystery gives it great range, and the power for its symbolism to brand any aspect of human life. It makes the mystery endlessly fascinating because it carries so many lines of text, so much magic. The beautiful flower, the thorns, the death of beauty and its subsequent resurrection are easily seen, so we can understand the rudimentary representation roses make of life and death, of transience, and even the bloody red rose of sacrifice. The circle that appears in the face of the rose, especially those ancient types we now call species roses, is another mystery, as is the fact that the single, simple blooms boast just five petals to their shallow cup, petals that describe the circle, pure and simple. So rose symbolism moves beyond the real to the abstract world of geometric shapes and numbers, the signs of magic and of power that form a framework behind the incantations and ritual of all religions. The circle, fundamental shape of womanhood, in turn the shape of the moon, the pregnant globe, is the shape of the rose flower. It has five petals, the number of fingers on a hand, or the five appendages of the body; legs, arms and head.

Spooky stuff, especially when you notice another mysterious plant, the apple, with which Eve committed original sin, also has a five-petal flower, and five pips arranged in the shape of a star. There is a botanic family link between apples and roses, hence the similar flower, and both share a place in 'beginning' myths. Apples were there in the garden many call Eden, and were the reason, if you ignore Eve's role,

Sweet Briar
Vivian Ward

that humans were banished from paradise. Ever since, dreams of that secret hidden garden that holds the answers to the mysteries of life have persisted, and the secret garden idea lies as deep within us as does that of the rose mystery.

Because so many of our spiritual roots are in the Middle East, we dream of gardens as the desert peoples made them; walled and orderly, from which refreshing water, life itself, springs. We even give these fantastic places a Persian name, paradise, and within their walls, some would say in pride of place, is the rose, the symbol of perfect beauty, beauty of the soul and of the heart, beauty through which we strive to gain release from real pain and death. Here the rose is elevated to become a gateway for the spirit, a way into paradise. The great Renaissance poet Dante Alighieri described his particular vision of the rose in paradise in his epic poem, *Divina Commedia*. His love, Beatrice is dead, taken by God to heaven, and there she is his guide on a profoundly spiritual journey, culminating in a stupendous vision:

> *In the form then of a pure white rose*
> *the holy host was shown to me*
> *which in His own blood Christ made his bride.*

> Paradiso 31

That is as powerful as poetic rose allegory gets, and indeed Dante's work is the first great rent in the orderly spiritual cloak that shielded Roman Catholics from the rose mystery's extreme. Through that rip came a flood of light that is now called the Renaissance, a spiritual and artistic surge of energy that returned pagan passions to centre stage and, as had been the case in ancient Greece and Rome, gave artists scope to play again with roses and their multifarious implications.

And play they did; many of our strongest images of classical deities were made by Renaissance artists, and perhaps the most striking is Botticelli's Venus, riding a scallop shell ashore on her sire's foam, and his rendering of Flora herself, emerging with spring from the dark forest of winter. Both paintings are rich with roses, either awash in the sea about Venus, or clutched by Flora in a bundle at her lap, spilling out across the reviving earth. Neither are soft images, rather they are charged with a disturbing undercurrent, a fierce sense of untamed spirit, of volatile power: the rose mystery's passion.

Not that roses had been neglected by thinkers before the Renaissance. In spite of sanctimonious attitudes to roses because of their long association with debauchery, the rose mystery was too powerful, too true, the great goddess idea too fundamental, to be ignored. After being briefly banished in the early days of the Christian Church, roses returned to the heart of common religion in Europe and the goddess, as Mary, Theotokis, Mother of God, took centre stage again, accompanied by the rose. The Marian cult returned to roses all their pagan glory, and more, until they became as pervasive in the Church as they were in the minds and spirits of ordinary people. They took their little symbolic rose gardens, circlets of beads, into church to assist their prayers, to help them keep count so that they may chant the right number of prayers to the Father, the Son or the Virgin, and these rosaries became tokens of their spirituality, to be carried always. They are the intimate, secret rose gardens of very private faith, personal tokens of the garden of enlightenment, a ring of roses that is the circle of life, the rose mystery encapsulated in form and in spirit.

Less secret is the rose emblazoned on numerous churches, a badge of fire that is a great, glowing symbol of the fertile Virgin rising in spectacular coloured glass before the westering sun. To stand before the vaulted chasm of Rheims or Chartres, or any of the monumental cathedrals, and be dazzled by the beauty of one of these great stone and glass circles is to feel the power of the rose in light, to recognise the depth of meaning that lies behind a pretty flower.

It is not surprising that the rose and Mary have assumed such power, or that the rose garden should have been a feature of monasteries as well as private castles. These secret gardens, in the tradi-

Dante's devotion to Beatrice, whom he made his guide through Paradise in *The Divine Comedy*, is one of literature's great loves, and in Blake's vision of the rose as Holy Host he has her revealing the rose in its most profound spiritual form, as the symbol of absolute spiritual love. Renaissance man's image of the Great Goddess, suitably adapted for Christian consumption.

"The Queen of Heaven in Glory", William Blake (Rare Books Room, Auckland Central City Library)

tion of the mystery, walled and hidden from the uninitiated, contained magical plants, not least of which was the fabulous Apothecary's Rose with its wondrous medicinal properties. For poets, the garden and the roses were, and remain, ripe with possibility. From the first French poems and the rustic English verse of Geoffrey Chaucer, poets have indulged themselves in roses. *Roman de la Rose*, a huge allegorical poem that spins its verses around a garden quest for the exquisite beauty of rosy perfection, could well be called the beginning of poetry for both the French and English. Written by two thirteenth-century French poets its story of quest and beauty was universal, and its influence reached into Chaucer's England, where the use of allegory, and roses, was honed to perfection by Spenser and Shakespeare.

And so on through poets, painters and other artists to the clamouring of a modern culture where boundaries have faded, where some aspects of the rose mystery may have been lost, but where the symbolic rose remains as strong and virile as ever, if less understood than it was. The world now is cluttered with cheap roses, from Guns'n'Roses to Roses chocolates, the mystery plastered thick on screens and pages to encourage sales; cheap mystery.

But roses fight on in 'Aotearoa', a rose as steamy as Aphrodite ever was, a full frontal rose that returns us to its essential character. And so the endless rhythm is maintained, as Gertrude Stein acknowledged in her deceptively simple, circular phrase, 'A rose is just a rose, is just a rose...'

The Wilton Diptych was used by Richard II as an icon of the divine validation of his rule; the King carried it with him wherever he went. On this right-hand panel, the Virgin and Child are depicted with white roses prominent at the Virgin's feet; perhaps symbols of the Virgin, or even the badge of Richard's worldly power.

The white rose had already been used as a badge of kingship, at least since Edward I and possibly longer, and its pure image certainly suited the saintly Kings, Edmund and Edward, whose legitimacy Richard invokes in this painting.

"The Wilton Diptych" Artist unknown (Reproduced by courtesy of the Trustees, The National Gallery, London)

2 Garden roots

No man knows
Through what wild centuries
Roves back the rose.

All That's Past, *Walter de la Mare*

There is a story that Britain was named Albion by the invading Roman legions because of the white abundance of Alba roses that they found growing there when they arrived. A nice tale, especially in a country that now calls the rose its own, and while it may not be true it does serve to illustrate how misty our knowledge of rose history is. As we proceed down this long and fragrant path from the earliest species roses to today's sophisticated cosmopolitans, it is worth noting that while we may be enchanted by the romance of it all, we are unlikely to be persuaded by a stack of unequivocal facts. The mystery has served to blur the outlines of reality, and often legend is the only history we have.

Roses are great travellers, and the New Zealand history of roses has more journeys in it than most, simply because we are further away from the beginning. Home for wild roses stretches across the Northern Hemisphere, generally avoiding the tropics with the exception of a few south-east Asian species that venture close to the equator in their natural ramblings. Those roses with the oldest pedigree are probably the subgenus *Rosa hulthemia*, which appropriately originate in the area south and east of the Caucusus mountains, east of the Caspian Sea. Coincidentally, this is also a region that seeded much of Western civilisation with its wandering humanity. A fertile ground for breeding mystery, and a good beginning for a saga of travel.

R. hulthemia, when it was taken west into the fertile basin of the Tigris and Euphrates Rivers, would have travelled well and flourished in its new home, and it just may have been the first rose to assume fertility symbolism in the early rituals of this ancient breeding ground of civilisations. Those two great rivers nurtured empires from the earliest Sumerian to the Persian, developing in their city states agriculture and gardens, writing and bureaucracy, and adding layers to the rose mystery as travellers from east and west became the first to be attracted by city glitter. There mixed a cosmopolitan brew of ideas, trade, language, magic, gods, animals, plants, religion and war, and in the ferment recognisable versions of the oldest known rose species — *R. canina*, *R. gallica*, *R. foetida* and *R. damescena* — could be found in the gardens of those first cities.

These four species are important players in the romance that history has made of the roses' story, and with all three travel is a recurrent theme. Venerable *R. gallica* lingers in the background of so many of the roses bred in the last century it could be comfortably called the mother of rose invention, if not the mother of roses. It was acclimatised to the rigours of Persian religious ritual over 3000 years ago, and according to paintings that have survived from Minoan Crete had been adopted to an important position in that celebrated culture with its bulls and luxurious architecture by 1600 BC.

From Crete it was a short distance to Greece, and although *R. gallica* was probably well known there, as it was in the flourishing new kingdom of Egypt, the collapse of Minoan power scattered aspects of its higher rose culture to these neighbours. Power ebbed and flowed around the Mediterranean like the inner sea's tides, and trade between the kingdoms at its edge grew stronger. *R. gallica* and its sisters followed in the wake of armies and along the merchant routes, from the Tigris to Spain. Rose cultivation spread, and in Macedonia the exiled King Midas built gardens, which the early historian Herodotus visited on his travels

An image of fecundity emerging from the dark grove of winter, the pregnant goddess of springtime, her breasts entwined with roses, spills rose blooms onto the ground as she walks, so spreading the new season's life-force. Heavy with pagan symbolism, Botticelli's Renaissance masterpiece returns the rose to its oldest form, as a symbol of feminine fertility.

"La Primavera", Sandro Botticelli (Reproduced by courtesy of the Uffizi Gallery, Florence)

The Christian church elevated the rose as the symbol of Mary, Mother of God, Virgin Queen of Heaven. In the spectacular rose windows of Europe's great cathedrals, including Rheims Cathedral pictured here, this symbol reached its pinnacle. But it has also survived in the far more intimate guise of rosary beads, prayer counters that are also symbolic gardens of roses and circlets mimicking the ancient cycle of the rose mystery.

In another ostensibly Christian work loaded with pagan symbolism, this beautiful seventeenth-century painting shows the Virgin with a chaste lily, while the Christ child holds out a pink rose, symbol of martyrdom. In the basket, another rose, that of sorrow, awaits Mary on His future crucifixion.

"The Virgin and Child with Flowers", Carlo Dolci (Reproduced by courtesy of the Trustees, The National Gallery, London)

The greatest virgin/goddess symbol of British history, Elizabeth I ruled over a virile nation that was in the flush of creative innovation, and she promoted her own image as that of the Virgin Queen, spiritually wedded to her realm.

Tudor heraldry aside, she used the rose as her personal badge of (feminine) power, and in almost all portraits of her there is a rose pinned to her dress, or held in her hand. Her motto was *Rosa sine spina*, rose without thorns, and of all the Tudor monarchs, the rose symbol was hers; giving extra momentum in England to its already substantial mythology, just as the country was being forced away from Catholicism and its rose-encrusted cult of the Virgin Mary.

"Queen Elizabeth" attributed to Nicholas Hilliard (By courtesy of the National Portrait Gallery, London)

and recorded in the oldest remaining European writings on rose cultivation. The plants he mentioned were, according to some modern
experts who have studied his text, *R. gallica*, or maybe *R. damescena*.

That was towards the end of the fourth century BC, 200 years after
the great Babylonian king Nebuchadnezzar II created his fabulous
Hanging Gardens. While little evidence remains of their glory, these
amazing gardens on the roofs of Nebuchadnezzar's royal palace almost
certainly contained roses and remained one of the wonders of the
ancient world until they were partially destroyed by King Darius during
his suppression of a Babylonian revolt against his Persian empire in 482
BC. By then, roses had passed through the hands of Greeks living in
Persian Asia Minor to their homeland, and the gardens of Midas where
Herodotus saw them.

Herodotus' comments were the first, but most certainly not the last
word on roses. By the time of Christ rose literature had recorded the
spread and domestication of roses in Chinese as well as Middle Eastern
and European languages. Almost 2000 years before Chinese rose developments influenced European gardens, Confucius noted that there
were 600 works on the rose in the Emperor's library. This was before 500
BC, by which time the process of hybridisation and domestication,
which has virtually eliminated wild roses from China, was well
advanced.

In Greece, the rose mystery was already well established and
as Aphrodite's importance increased, and she rose up the ladder of
pantheon society, the love rituals she demanded made the fragrant,
pretty rose blooms more common. The Greeks, however, did not garden
as avidly as the 'paradise' makers of Persia, the goddess's original home,
but their intellectual vigour, in works such as Theophrastus' *Historia
Plantarum*, provided knowledge with which the Roman and Egyptian
gardeners who succeeded them could more fully realise the potential
of floriculture.

The plant world of classical Greece was altogether more natural
and unshaped than that of Rome, where the control of nature was

practised with great relish. Egypt harvested roses for winter markets in the Roman Empire's mercantile flush, and Rome itself grew fields of roses to supply burgeoning religious and social demand. By this time, *R. damescena* in its two forms was proving invaluable as a means of extending the supply period for as long as possible. Roman gardeners, competing with the Egyptians whose method of transporting fresh roses across the Mediterranean by sail and slave oar has never been rediscovered, forced roses to either hold back their flowers or bring them on early. With the use of devices such as warm water irrigation and the original glasshouses to create special micro climates, they met the needs of their increasingly demanding customers.

In these circumstances, the Summer Damask (*R.* x *damescena*) and Autumn Damask (*R. damescena bifera*) had the advantage of flowering naturally at different times, spreading the supply of blooms over a wider summer season. It was probably these roses that gave the famous rose-growing centre of Paestum its reputation for producing two flushes in one season.

Sited on the warm plains beside the Gulf of Salerno, 100 kilometres south of Naples, Paestum is suitably balmy and in spite of the nearby swamps, which proved problematic at times and ultimately saw the rose farms move elsewhere, was a perfect climate for rose growing. It is probable that Gallicas as well as Damasks, and most other known varieties from throughout the Empire, were grown there, with travellers bringing new types back to Italy as the legions extended the range of *pax romana*. Roman knowledge of rose culture would have certainly developed under such conditions, beyond the scope of Theophrastus' writings, and private gardening was enhanced by a consequent advance in floricultural skill.

The decline of Rome also saw the decline of commercial floriculture from its relatively advanced Roman state, and commercial rose growing of any consequence effectively disappeared from Europe for 800 years, until the French town of Provins became the centre for a new rose industry in the eleventh century. In spite of this lack of substantial

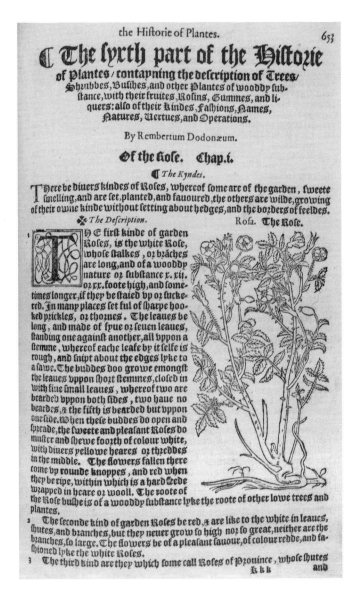

Woodcut of rose plant from Dodoens, *A Nievve Herball,* English edition published 1578.

(Rare Books Room, Auckland Central City Library)

gardens, small plots were maintained in rare cases when power and wealth could sustain such an indulgence. This was primarily within church orders, which valued knowledge enough to retain some of the faded Empire's gardening expertise and which needed supplies of fresh herbs and other plants to sustain their apothecary role, their daily diet and their churches' need for decoration.

Because of the Church and its early doctrines that excluded the rose symbol, the medieval age of Europe was a time when the rose was sustained by its mystery. It was a time of insecurity as families fought for power in their own lands; the world was in a state of perpetual turmoil, and few were safe from pillaging mercenaries, savage taxes, or the ravages of plague. It was a time when the garden offered an intimate world that epitomised peace, even for the multitude for whom the garden was an unattainable luxury.

For those who could afford a garden, a hidden place within castle walls or the cloistered sanctuary of a monastery, it offered succour through its calm beauty, and in the medicinal value of its plants. Gardens were a valuable symbol of security, even for powerful lords who had control over their own armies and castles in which to rest from the threat of a dangerous world, and roses were probably the most important plants in those gardens. They were beautiful, if not as spectacular as modern roses, fragrant, and loaded with the symbolism of hope that had meaning for superstitious people.

Hard times worked in favour of the rose, if only because its hardiness as a plant ensured its survival when other plants died through neglect or destruction. Most significantly, roses' association with love ensured their value to an age that elevated personal love to a spiritual plane that challenged contemporary religion. The oldest medieval myths tell of love that challenged pain, warfare, exile, the social confines of marriage, and even death; great love stories that tell of how private love stood against the establishment, stories that still survive — Tristan and Iseult, Lancelot and Guenivere. They were the stories sung by troubadours, those original poets of courtly love who travelled southern France singing love's praises.

In spite of the best efforts of the medieval establishment, however, ideas of personal love and the rose as its symbol remained and flourished. The role of the rose secured it a pre-eminent position in the medieval garden and the gardens that followed. The modern garden is a direct descendant of the walled enclave created for private enjoyment and solace, just as modern concepts of love are a consequence of the emotional individuality celebrated by the troubadours.

The Byzantine Church, before its split with Rome, had served as a conduit through which many of the garden concepts of the East passed into Europe. The schisms that kept Europe confused for centuries served to hide much of the detail of this flow of knowledge, but the rich garden symbolism of the late medieval poem, *Roman de la Rose*, and the vibrant colours of manuscript illumination, shows gardens obviously influenced by the Persian legacy.

Attributed spiritual power, it is not surprising that roses were as important in medicine as they were in art, at a time when the power to heal was an intrinsic quality of princes, holy figures and religious symbols. *R. gallica* was well known in medieval Europe as the Apothecary's Rose. Its red petals, claimed as a cure for an amazing variety of ills, also preserved their remarkable perfume when dried, in itself a soothing characteristic.

R. gallica's petals were an understandable part of medieval medicine, religion, art, and consequently commerce, a commonplace fact of European life in the middle ages. The red of Gallica was also juxtaposed by gardeners with the virgin white of the Alba rose, which legend says gave Britain its name, and *R. x alba* was as well known at the time as *R. gallica*, with its white symbolism and spiritual nuances. This was especially the case in England, where the Alba rose had been used at least since the Roman occupation. It is a member of the tough *R. canina* family, a breed hardy enough to have acclimatised to the harsher north so easily that it was considered a native by the time legends about its origins were passed around in Imperial Rome. Today, no expert can be sure just where its origins lie, but it has been present throughout Europe for generations and may be the product of chance meetings between *R. canina* and *R. gallica* in some forgotten place and time.

Other hardy types were also making their presence felt in medieval gardens, with the Eglantine's enchanting apple-tinted fragrance and sweet pink flowers attracting much support. *R. eglanteria*, was, and is, commonly called Sweet Briar, a reference to the charming simplicity of its flowers and fragrance. It has an important part to play in the history of New Zealand roses, partially a reflection of the ease with which it has fitted into the rural English countryside for at least a thousand years.

Eglantine and Alba are tough, but roses such as *R. gallica* and the Damasks did not wander out from their medieval garden walls for generations. Magic took their names abroad: the magic that claimed their power in cures, and cleverly used their fragrances in perfumes for which the recipes were secretly held. Called red, or rose, those original Gallicas are in fact pink, but the value of their scent remains undeniable, and was especially prized in an age when the lack of public and personal hygiene reduced most settlements and people to a particularly smelly state. Technological shortfall forced people to resort to natural remedies, and the fragrant properties of Gallica petals were further enhanced by

BUT·STOOD·TURN'D·SIDEWAYS; LISTENING,

The popular Arthurian legends absorbed many of the pagan myths, frequently Celtic in origin, that preceded Christianity. Forbidden love was one of these, finding form in the Lancelot and Guinevere, and Tristan and Iseult stories that also carry many of the ideas of courtly love from later periods. Illustrations of the stories, albeit from a much later time, are rich in symbolic roses, representing pain and transience as much as love and passion.
"The Defence of Guinevere" (Rare Books Room, Auckland Central City Library)

their increased intensity when dried. They were more than a breath of fresh air in the stifling summer streets of Paris or London, festering with open drains and the press of unwashed thousands.

Fragrance and gardens were an escape for the wealthy. There were few, if any, private gardens that belonged to those who worked the land, or who struggled in towns and cities in the artisan world. But if beauty was a luxury to the majority, who gained no concessions from a harsh system based on land ownership, in the rose it was also a sign of hope.

Still, with dukes and princes richer often than emperors or kings, and Europe's cities gathered about the glow of courtly indulgence and fashion, there was a healthy profit to be had in mercantile arrangements with those for whom cost was no object. Bakers and butchers struggled, but luxury goods were in demand and what greater luxury than the rose, from which rich perfumes and oils were made, and medicines extracted to soothe the ruling brow. Count Thibaut IV of Champagne and Navarre was not a man to let the main chance go by, and he set about establishing healthy industries for both roses and wine within his domain. No doubt the purpose was to increase his already considerable wealth and power, but it had the happy consequence of also improving the welfare of his subjects.

In Thibaut's honour they created a legend that credits his introduction of the Rose of Provins into Europe. The story claims he carried cuttings, hips or even plants of this now-famous rose in his luggage all the way from Damascus. At the same time he was also transporting another valuable plant, the chardonnay vine. While these feats are not impossible, they are highly unlikely; modern investigation reveals that both the Rose of Provins and chardonnay grapes were known in France, if not widely used, before Thibaut's undoubtedly difficult return from the seventh crusade. Although there is more romance than reality to the tale, its source lies in the efforts made by this remarkable ruler to establish sound economies in his lands, efforts that laid the foundations of two formidable industries that have since become synonymous with France and luxury: perfume and Champagne.

The Rose of Provins is not a Damask rose, as the legend suggests, but the famous Apothecary's Rose, *R. gallica officinalis*. The industry that Thibaut IV established at Provins during the thirteenth century continues to flourish in the picturesque valley of the Seine, south-east of Paris, which remains one of the most important and technologically advanced rose growing and breeding centres in the world. The fame of Provins roses, even within the lifetime of the Count, spread throughout Europe, and the French have ever since quite reasonably claimed the rose as their own flower, as much as they claim passion and perfume as their own creations.

The English disagree. The English rose has a history at least as legendary, if not as old, as that of France. The Gallica roses may be named after ancient Gaul, where the Romans noted their abundance, but England has the equally romantic legend of Albion's white roses, and the concept of beauty allegorically named the 'English rose'. Perhaps the brief, virginal blush of Eglantine, the Sweet Briar, prompted this description, or maybe the tender pink of an ancient Alba called Celeste.

The English even have a tale, carefully documented in the tradition of British bureaucracy, of a lord returning from a crusade inspired by the rose mystery. King Edward I came back from Acre in 1272 and promptly embarked on a promotion of the rose within his country. He adopted a golden rose as his badge, planted roses in that bleak citadel, the Tower of London, and in his Bill of Medicines produced in 1306 mentions a Damask rose, which was probably the Apothecary's Rose, the identity of which was confused by tales told of warriors returning from Damascus laden with botanic booty.

Edward I was one of the greatest English monarchs, as adept at government as he was at war. His rose badge set a precedent, and in seeking to emulate the image of relative peace and order Edward's rule evoked, the rose became a popular emblem with the powerful families who struggled amongst each other for supremacy in the period after his reign. This turmoil reached its nasty peak 200 years later with the Wars of the Roses, named after the badges of the leading parties, the white

Banksiae alba-plena
Vivian Ward

rose of York and the red of Lancaster, neither of which was to ultimately become established as the royal rose of England.

There are claims that the white Alba rose is the rose of York, as the red rose of Lancaster is a Gallica, but while these are attractive notions for rose enthusiasts, it is unlikely that there are close botanical associations between real roses and the coats of arms of those warring parties. The adoption of the rose as a heraldic symbol was, as revealed in the citation to the grant of a coat of arms to Eton College in 1449, to '…bring forth the rightest flowers redolent in every kind of science to which also, that we might impart something of regal nobility…' It seems entirely appropriate, then, that the rose should be adopted by a family with aspirations to the throne, especially in the wake of Edward I, and its use by the protagonists in the famous wars simply serves to endorse the concept of the rose symbol's 'regal nobility'.

It is symbolic also that the Wars of the Roses ended with the Tudors, whose symbol of reconciliation was a double rose, with the white inside the red. It was under the Tudor rose that England entered the Renaissance and acquired the economic and creative power, especially in science and literature, that was to spread the English rose around

Roses, only partly symbolic, show up as recognisable domestic decoration in this Victorian view of Tudor England. (Rare Books Room, Auckland Central City Library)

the world. Under the Tudor rose Francis Drake was the first Englishman to broach the Pacific and travel the whole world, establishing a precedent that would be followed by later generations of Englishmen, none greater than Captain James Cook, the genius navigator who was the first bearer of the rose mystery to New Zealand, in spirit if not in fact.

Drake's Queen, Elizabeth I, also ruled while the brilliance of Shakespeare and Spenser permanently embroidered the rose mystery into the heart of English literature. *The Faerie Queene* was written for and about Elizabeth, the mother of English glory, who added to the rose mystery a special Tudor touch by taking as her personal emblem the thornless rose, symbol of the Virgin Mary.

If literature has sustained the rose mystery, science made an art of the rose alone. In bridging the gap between belief and empirical science, luck again played an important part. The invention of the printing press created books that were accessible to great numbers of readers, which seized learning from the powerful and spread it about a larger population. They gave the science of plants and gardening a popularity that was unprecedented, fostering a quest for knowledge that

The grand contrived vistas of Versailles set the 'high art' gardens of Europe's landed gentry, including the British, beyond popular gardening. There were still places for roses, however, within the exotic formality of the whole.

opened up the botanic world. Even with historical hindsight, it is difficult to comprehend the effect books had on science, especially for accessible areas of study such as botany, which occupied the world in which most new readers lived.

Plants became objects of study; gardens became opportunities to use new knowledge in the creation of personal worlds of botanic understanding. Gardens moved from castles and monasteries to less palatial private homes, and in England the nation's wealth was building a sizeable middle class that had the time and money to indulge in this newly fashionable pursuit. Naturally, the rose had a place; honoured by poets and royalty, acknowledged by the church, it was a place at the centre of the garden. What is remarkable is that while other plants lost their status as science sought out the bizarre and diverse, the romantic rose maintained its position and, with time and luck, enhanced it.

Increased interest in the rose's botanic make-up revealed just how diverse its background was, and while it was generally assumed to be a common plant, there seems to have been enough mystery and diversity to keep interest high just when the attention of gardeners was being attracted by more exotic plants. Gallicas, Albas, Dog Roses, Eglantine, Damasks — they all found places, and were grown in a number of ways which their earlier monastic and princely masters had not considered appropriate to their strict enclosures and courtly sites. It became a time of quest, for knowledge, understanding, discovery and for personal expression; it was a time of opportunity for people whose names history has not recorded, but who have contributed a great deal to the celebration of roses through their inquisitive botany.

The search for knowledge also became a search for classification and habit, as well as genealogy and origins. In the process the Dutch created an entirely new rose, *R. centifolia*, the legendary hundred-petalled rose, with a reputation almost as old as roses. This rose marked a new beginning; Europe's introduction to hybridisation through which the form of the rose was to be completely changed. From now on the rose became more the flower of humans, less the flower of gods.

3 British nursery

Old-fashioned roses, large blooms ruffed by layers of petals, are not as old nor as natural as many would have us believe. Like so much of the rose story, they are as ripe with mystery and paradox as any other chapter; they mark not a past age of grace and natural beauty but the first rose experience of the tidy world of science.

The rose was an early candidate for manipulation by botanists. It was a well-known plant, readily available in a number of forms, was commercially grown, and had an image that was as capable of influencing budding scientists as much as artists. For the rose story, the creation of *Rosa x centifolia* was a spectacular success, for it was the embodiment of the sumptuous rose of legend which until then real roses had failed to match. Coming up with Centifolias so quickly was for early experimenters like finding the Holy Grail at the front gate on the first morning of the quest, a precedent that transported roses effortlessly into the world of science. It also made the rose plant as popular as the rose mystery, by the simple process of making a dream come true.

R. x *centifolia* is, in fact and in form, the rose that bridges the gap between the old world of tamed wild roses and religious symbolism, and the new world's fashioned domestic roses and artistic allegory. In one step the rose gardeners responsible proved that science, even in its most rudimentary form, could enhance romance by creating new roses to suit the oldest stories, and so delivered roses into the popular gardens that were fast replacing the secret places of privilege. It does not seem to have mattered that an equivalent breeding success was not achieved for another 200 years; the popularity of Centifolias lasted long enough for them to be important components in the colonisation of New Zealand 12 generations after they first appeared.

The exact origin of the Centifolias is unknown, as there are almost no records of the methods used to produce them or their specific parentage. While recent genetic investigation has revealed that there are strains of three of the original roses — R. *gallica,* R. *canina* and R. *damescena* — as well as R. *phoenicia* and R. *moschata* in their lineage, this is probably as close as we will ever get to the details of their breeding. All of these archaic rose species were widely spread throughout medieval Europe, and all would have been growing in the famous gardens that had been established in the United Provinces of the Netherlands by the late sixteenth century. It was in those gardens that Centifolias were first bred, but where, and by whom, will always remain part of the rose mystery.

The Dutch tradition of rose growing was well established by the time Centifolias appeared. The fact that no record of Centifolias' breeding remains can partly be blamed on a lack of precise knowledge by the gardeners themselves about what they were doing, particularly when this involved plant genetics. Most likely the new rose was a product of an organised accident, from beds in which roses of every known species were mixed together in the knowledge that new types would emerge. It was rough science born of ignorance and enthusiasm, for it was still

200 years before the first planned rose breeding would produce an intended hybrid, but it was obviously effective, even if it could not be repeated exactly.

It is an example of the remarkable luck of roses that from such haphazard practices there was any substantial success at all, never mind a new rose to enchant botanists and gardeners with its legendary hundred petals, with the added bonuses of expansive fragrance and fine colouring. It is not surprising this rose quickly joined the other garden roses as a status symbol for the new generation of private gardeners.

As gardens flourished, so too did roses and the rose mystery — a point made clear in the first botanic publications, which made important contact between scientists and gardeners. In one of the most famous of these, Gerard's *Herball* of 1597, John Gerard is unequivocal in his introduction to the section on roses: '...the Rose doth deserve the chiefest and most principall place among all flours whatsoever, beeing not onely esteemed for his beautie, vertues, and his fragrant odorisroue smell.' Praise indeed in a book that contains descriptions of over 2000 plants, only 18 of which are roses.

Herbals like Gerard's were the first botanic publications, and also continued the tradition of herbal medicine. The early herbals were in fact a rather incongruous mixture of scientific observation, superstition, and rudimentary medicine, which, while introducing the science of botanic classification to rose growing, retained a hold on the more spiritual forms of rose symbolism. It was a diversity that showed how influential established rose images were in defining its future role, but by following the descriptions of roses in a succession of leading herbals it is possible to see how science gradually excluded myth from pharmacy, until herbals, medical and botanic texts became entirely separate areas of knowledge and publishing.

Appropriately, given the Centifolia connection, one of the first important herbals published in England was a translation of *A Nievve Herball or a Historie of Plantes*, written by the renowned Dutch botanist Rembert Dodoens. Printed in England in 1578 and dedicated to Queen

Elizabeth I, it was published before the death of Dodoens, who died in 1585, and predates Gerard by 20 years. Although of Dutch origin, it does not mention *R. x centifolia* at all, indicating that the new variety had not appeared when it was written. Gerard, however, included Centifolia, which he called *R. hollandica*, and the 'Great Holland Rose, commonly called the Great Province Rose', suggesting that *R. x centifolia* most probably emerged in the period between 1570 and 1597.

Many of the rose descriptions used by Dodoens suggest that his book influenced Gerard, and as a notably scientific gardener it is probable that Gerard had a copy. Dodoens classified roses into ten categories, six tame and four wild, a division Gerard also made. The tame roses are '…of the garden, sweete smelling, and are set, planted and favoured', while the wild roses are 'growing of their own kinde without setting about hedges, and the borders of fields.'

Of those which can be accurately identified from the descriptions, the six garden roses included Alba, Gallica, Damask and Musk roses; a rose Dodoens called the 'Caffia or Canel Rose' could possibly be *R. majalis*, the Cinnamon Rose. Eglantine, or Sweet Briar, which was listed as a wild rose, was also mentioned as a suitable plant for the garden, while the remaining three — yellow roses (*R. foetida*), *R. canina* and *R. spinosa* (*R. pimpinellifolia*) — Dodoens thought suitable only for hedgerows and other non-garden uses.

As interesting as these descriptions are, what is particularly revealing about the botanical rose entries is that they occupy less of Dodoens's text than do the medicinal and pharmaceutical values of roses. Roses, he claimed, 'especially of them that are reddist, or the infusion or decoction of them is of the kinde of soft and gentle medicines, which loose and open the belly and may be taken without danger. It purgeth downward cholerique humours and openeth the stoppings of the liver, strengthening and clensing the same also it is good against hoate fevers and against the Jaunders.'

Powerful stuff. Dodoens went on to list a range of rose medicines that were mostly effective in cases where there was some association

The sexual innuendo in this caricature from Rowlandson's "The Dance of Life" is enhanced by the less than subtle symbolism of the roses. "He Plays His Lively Court", Thomas Rowlandson (Rare Books Room, Auckland Central City Library)

between the malady and the ancient properties attributed to roses by mythology. What he was actually recording were spiritual cures, when ascribed rose properties corresponded to those parts of the human anatomy accorded similar mythical functions. The heart, breasts and genitals were regular beneficiaries of this 'medicine', and dried rose petals when 'boyled' in wine were said to be 'good against . . . the Mother or Women's secretes, eyther poured in or annoyted with a feather.' Not exactly scientifically collected information, but an indication of the use of roses in Elizabethan England and a sign of the rose mystery's influence on the most cultivated minds of the day.

Herbals continued to make great use of the rose mystery, even when botanic publications such as the excellent, illustrated *Florilegeum* produced by the Dutch gardener, Emaneul Sweerts, as early as 1612, began to concentrate on botany. Nicholas Culpepper's claim in his 1681 herbal, *The English Physitian Enlarged, with 369 Medicines made of English Herbs*, that 'Red roses strengthen the heart' would surely be of interest to the Heart Foundation if this applied to the physical, not the emotional, organ. Culpepper actually abandoned any attempt at a scientific description of roses: 'there is no need to describe them they are so common'. Instead he simply listed three types — Garden roses, Wild roses, and Bryars — and placed a selection under the influence of various mythic and divine figures: 'Red Roses under Jupiter, Damask under Venus, White under the moon, and Provence under the King of France.'

By the middle of the next century there seems to have been

little change in the reliance on rose mythology in newly published herbals, which had regressed if anything from the scientific position established by Dodoens. *The Garden of Health* by William Langham, published in 1769, commits eight and a half pages to rose remedies, with 127 specific medicinal entries. While he described the rose as 'chiefe of all flowers', Langham paid little attention to anything other than archaic apothecarian myth, and by this time herbals seem to have become an anachronism as the sciences of botany and medicine stimulated more specific publishing.

In 1752, Philip Miller, gardener at the famous Chelsea Physick Garden, published the sixth edition of his *Gardener's Dictionary*, which included in its remarkable list of garden plants the names of 26 roses. It was a landmark book in the history of garden publishing, for it was the first remotely accurate attempt at classifying garden varieties and it gave considerable substance to the expanding science of botany as it was applied to gardening. His work would be taken up again in France at the turn of the century, and his influence felt by New Zealand's colonial rose growers as they sought to follow European fashion a hundred years later.

By the nineteenth century, herbals had dropped all reference to the old world of herbal and spiritual healing and, in deference to the success of garden books, rose sections had become insignificant. The *New Family Herbal* of 1810, by botany lecturer Dr Robert John Thornton, has less than a page given to rose remedies, and although the author mentioned Gallica, Damask and Dog Roses, and, strangely, called Damasks Centifolias, he listed the most favourable attributes of rose preparations as being simply mildness, attractive aroma and pretty colour. Roses, it seems, had at last been replaced by more scientifically proven medicines and rose publishing was about to acquire its own identity.

The listing of descriptions and classifying plants accordingly is the basis of the science of botany, and Dodoens's sixteenth-century work was botanic pioneering at its most basic. The precise, intricate and at times convoluted classification of roses and other plants that absorbs modern botanists is a consequence of books such as *A Nievve Herball*, a practice that seems to have little relevance to today's gardeners other than to maintain a trace of Latin in common language. Gardening books, however, also have their origins in the work of Dodoens and Gerard.

The early herbals distributed information about plants such as roses, which individuals could then apply to the development of their own gardens. The exclusive nature of gardening of previous times was in part due to the exclusivity of knowledge about plants, so books were as important to the popularising of roses as were creations such as *R. x centifolia*. In an earlier print-free age, the hundred-petalled rose would have become another secret garden mystery like the Damask, Gallica and Musk had been, and there would have been no such thing as the 'yeoman cottage gardener', to whom gardening writer Gertrude Jekyll later attributed the creation of the English cottage garden.

Elitist fashion, now deprived of exclusive possession of the rose garden, looked elsewhere for botanic entertainment and found it in the open vistas of 'English' landscape gardens. Created originally by William Kent, and refined by the genius of Capability Brown, these gardens were manipulated landscapes, requiring planting on a huge scale; their views consumed villages and demanded artificial lakes and other water features to complement carefully placed tree lines and copses. The aim was to cultivate a pictorially 'natural' English countryside for the delight of occupants of grand country houses and their visitors, a scheme in which the orderly arrangement of floral gardens had no place. Instead, the more intimate environments of such country gardens were planned to look as natural as possible, and roses were to be used only where they fitted contemporary concepts of rural England.

While Capability Brown and his aristocratic sponsors made this form of English gardening high art, the rest of England was enchanted by a more intimate form of gardening — one which made their homes attractive, and which allowed their growing interest in plants to be actively fulfilled. It was a time when most people in the British Isles were country dwellers, and gardens became an important aspect of family life, part of a British idyll that was to be recalled during the bleak years ahead. As the 'dark, satanic mills' of Britain's industrial muscle pressed in on the countryside, sucking people into urban slums, the memory of those times and gardens became dreams of hope.

The roses growing in these small private gardens of Georgian Britain included fat, lush Centifolias, which the British prosaically called cabbage roses, as well as other 'garden' roses mentioned by both Dodoens and Gerard: Albas, Damasks and Gallicas. It was a small but interesting collection, made up almost entirely of plants that had legendary links with British history, another sign of the rose mystery at work. Of the Albas, the one known as the White Rose of York, *R.* x *alba*, has a fine English legend attached that made it most popular, especially, we may expect, in Yorkshire. Also named after the House of York is *R. canina* x *R. gallica*, a double white rose more commonly called the Jacobite Rose, or Bonnie Prince Charlie's Rose, after the Young Pretender who used it as his emblem. Although this legend remains one of the few that can be verified, this rose is no longer as popular as it once was, but it can still be found throughout Britain in country gardens.

An altogether more sensual association than that offered by British civil wars was attributed to another favoured Alba, Maiden's Blush, a deliciously perfumed flower, plump with sweetly pink petals. Known to the French as Cuisse de Nymphe, or Nymph's Thigh, the name may have been sterilised by English propriety, but its evocative form and fragrance kept it a favourite amongst generations of otherwise proper gardeners. It is probably the most common of the genuinely old roses found in English gardens today.

Maintaining the theme of British history is the Damask York and Lancaster Rose, so called because it does not seem to be able to make up its mind whether to be pink or white. Sometimes the pretty semi-double flowers are both, or pink and white appear side by side on the same head. An exercise in diplomacy that the Houses of York and

The archetypal English cottage garden with roses around the door, an image that has been re-made in so many of New Zealand's private gardens.
"The Deserted Village" (Rare Books Room, Auckland Central City Library)

Lancaster never quite managed. Another prominent member of the Damask family, known at the time as the Monthly Rose because of its rare, regular flowering habit, was the Autumn Damask, which remained in bloom when others had faded and gone. With a pretty pink flower and a wonderful scent when dried, it was used for its fragrance long after summer was over.

Moss roses, scions of the Centifolias, were introduced to Britain in 1727 by Philip Miller, author of the *Gardener's Dictionary*, to the Chelsea Physick Garden. These became as popular as their parent plant. Both types have the big, globular flowers packed with petals that attracted the cabbage rose tag, but the Moss roses have a fuzz of bristly growths on their stems and calyxes to distinguish them from the Centifolias.

Gallicas too had an important place in the gardens of eighteenth-century Britain, and carried with them that strong association with British history that was so important for success in the united king-doms, in spite of their foreign family name. The crimson flowers attracted the name Red Rose of Lancaster in an ongoing reference to the old civil war that Shakespeare popularised, and which remains indelibly bound to garden roses. It is unlikely that the reference is accurate, in spite of attempts by some British gardening writers to sustain the romance, but it managed to keep this rose a favourite in Britain as well as France, where it is known as the Double French Rose.

Rosa Mundi from Curtis'
Garden Magazine.
Overlaid with the legend
of King Henry II's
mistress Rosamund, this
rose holds aspects of both
British legend and the
threatening sexuality of
the even older rose
mystery.
(Rare Books Room, Auckland
Central City Library)

Officially *R. gallica officinalis*, this important rose is both the Apothecary's Rose and Rose of Provins, and as we have seen is one of the heros of rose history.

The remarkable striped flowers of *R. gallica versicolor*, or Rosa Mundi, have a slightly more risqué legend than is normally attached to roses popular in England. The story is that they were named after Fair Rosamund, the mistress of King Henry II. Rosamund was kept in a house accessible only through a particularly complex maze, to keep her safe from the Queen's jealousy. Queen Eleanor, in the tradition of Greek hero Theseus solving the puzzle of the Cretan labyrinth, cracked the maze and poisoned her rival. The storyline suggests that the legend may be a good deal older than Rosa Mundi, or Rosamund, but has had a rearrangement of characters to suit English conditions. Rosa Mundi is a very old rose indeed, even as old, in England at least, as the Rose of Provins of which it is said to be a sport, or deviant child.

Perhaps a more sumptuous royal legend could have been woven about another genuinely old Gallica, the Old Velvet Rose, for its velvet red petals and crown of golden stamens make a fine regal display. However, in keeping with the names Maiden's Blush and the cabbage rose, the British seem to persistently avoid the obvious nature of roses' sensual form and strong colour, a tradition that seems to survive in the neutered watercolour washes that so frequently pose as rose portraits today.

Along with the Scotch or Burnet Rose of the R. *pimpinellifolia* family, this makes up a small list, containing no more than a dozen roses, which, with wild Dog Roses and Eglantine in the hedges, were available to those gardeners who created the traditional English cottage gardens now much promoted in literature and marketing mythology. These roses are certainly old-fashioned, some being at least 2000 years old, probably more, and their form and fragrance can be identified in many of the so-called old-fashioned roses promoted today. More importantly, they are the ancestors of modern roses, in which their characters also survive, the first of which was that evocation of an ancient dream, Centifolia.

The two great British revolutions, agricultural and industrial, all but destroyed the artisan rural environment in which these gardens were made. But in their destruction they made the garden a legend, at the heart of which is the ideal of having a personal relationship with a specific piece of land, a concept which survives in English-speaking people almost everywhere. The garden legend, in which the rose mystery plays a fundamental part, is for most people the only possible realisation of this ideal, and as such had a profound influence on the wave of emigration that took British hopefuls out to settle the wildest edges of the liveable world.

New Zealand was perhaps the most extreme edge, but the emigrants who came brought with them dreams made in Britain, dreams infused by the idealistic bond between people and private land. Their ideal world had cottage gardens with roses in them; there were roses in their churches, in their medicines, in the high culture of their literature and art, and in the popular cultures of love and home. The world they planned would be better than England, so the best English flower, the symbol of the nation's power and its fertile maidenhood and indeed its future, was an essential part of the plan.

Moss Rose
Vivian Ward

4 Cross-over

You have been my treasure, Rose Pilgrim,
Because of your beautiful name.
But because of your name I would not pamper you,
And I chose you to be planted in a difficult place,
In the path of the east wind;
Where at times, too, your roots might become thirsty,
Although I have a thirty foot hose.

You have thrived in spite of these disadvantages.
When your first shoots were battered by the spring storms,
Others pushed forth perseveringly.
You have been my treasure, Pilgrim Rose.

And you were up near the frontier, near the gateway,
So that when I come home, tired in the evening,
Home to my hill-garden, Rose Pilgrim,
You are the first flower I find there,
You are the very first flower, my Rose Pilgrim,
Pilgrim, my sweet rose.

Elect, *Mary Ursula Bethell*

The blur of mystery around which the romance of roses is woven is as much a part of the history of roses in New Zealand as it is of the greater rose story. Mystery and luck: together they gently weave roses into the Maori's first experiments with European culture, and European with Maori, until we cannot be sure which race it was that first brought roses here. The threads of this particular rose story cannot be retraced to an unequivocal source about

61

which historians can agree. This is as it should be for any mystery. How roses came here, why, and with whom, will never be known for sure.

It is not even possible, in the years when the seventeenth century became the eighteenth and New Zealand drew adventurers to its wild potential, to assume that the first New Zealand roses came from Europe; the ships that arrived here came via South America and South Africa, or from New South Wales, or even from China via the Dutch East Indies or some Pacific island. Even if the roses that did make it here were also to be found in Europe, there is some doubt as to the origins of the originals, or how they exactly got to Europe; it is possible that these same wanderers made it to New Zealand without going to Europe at all.

European rosarians were at this time being excited by regular arrivals from the great rose library of China, where all manner of enchanting rose phenomena were being discovered. These new plants were themselves stimulating additions to the rose grower's repertoire, and tempting introductions for breeders looking for rare plants to help satisfy the demand for unusual and wonderful new roses. It was the beginning of a new age of roses, and of rose breeding, with more variety than had ever been available to rosarians before.

In 1792 one of the first of these Oriental discoveries, a small hybrid rose with attractive crimson flowers, arrived in Europe from China courtesy of a director of the East India Company, Mr Gilbert Slater. The innovative British periodical, *Curtis's Botanical Magazine*, which had begun publishing just a short time before in 1787, was very enthusiastic about the newcomer in a profile written for Volume 8. This was published less than two years after the rose was first introduced by Mr Slater.

We are induced to consider the rose here represented as one of the most desirable plants in point of ornament ever introduced to this country; its flowers, large and in proportion to the plant are semi-double, and with great richness of colour unite a most delightful fragrance; they blossom during the whole of the year, more sparingly indeed in winter months; the shrub itself is more hardy than most greenhouse plants and will grow in so small a compass of earth it may be reared in a coffee cup; it is kept with the least possible trouble, and propagated without difficulty by cuttings or suckers.

The arrival of the China roses, especially Slater's Crimson China as this plant was subsequently named, had a profound effect on the rose gardening world, and on the future of rose growing in New Zealand. It is thought that the crossing of this pretty little rose with a Damask was the first step towards creating the large and influential Hybrid Perpetual family of roses, which was, after Centifolias, the second of the great modern rose families and particularly effective in the rose colonisation of New Zealand. Slater's Crimson China is also believed to be the first rose brought to New Zealand, although from where, and by whom, remains a mystery.

Perhaps the beginning of the New Zealand rose story lies in roses' luck and in the vision of Ruatara, an outstanding individual whose efforts on behalf of his people facilitated the planned introduction of European culture to New Zealand. A rangatira of the Te Hikitu hapu in the Bay of Islands, and nephew of the powerful Hongi Hika, Ruatara became interested in the world of white men, prompted no doubt by his contact with the sealers and whalers who frequently sought the protected anchorage and local trade of the Bay. In 1805, when only 18, he joined the crew of the whaling ship *Argo* in order to find out more about these foreign visitors. After a hard year working the New Zealand coast with a gang of the roughest characters European civilisation could provide, he arrived in Sydney, where his first experience of European settlement was the austere society of a convict colony.

Returning to the Bay of Islands, Ruatara's interest in things European seems to have been aroused rather than repelled. Less than a year later he again joined a whaler in the hope that he would make it to London, the place he had deduced from his contacts with British seamen, and in Sydney, to be the centre of the white world. There he planned to meet King George III, a logical expectation given his own distinguished position. After an especially difficult voyage, however, he was abandoned on the London docks without pay and with no more than the meanest clothing. He was ridiculed when he asked directions to the King's palace, and was summarily dispatched, sick, back to Sydney on the convict ship *Ann*, an experience that should have aroused hatred in him at least for his abusers if not all white people.

It was in 1809, and on board the *Ann*, that Ruatara met another cultural explorer heading south, Samuel Marsden. Marsden saw it would be in his interest to befriend a man whose influence could be of assistance, and whose support at this critical time probably did more to advance the future cause of European settlement in New Zealand than any other act of that ambitious cleric. Marsden, as well as being chaplain of the convict settlement at Botany Bay, also presided over the South Pacific activities of the Church Missionary Society, the branch of the Anglican Church whose function it was to convert heathens to Christianity. He probably considered Ruatara's presence on board to be Divine Providence, and cultivated a close relationship with the young Maori which deepened during Ruatara's protracted stay with Marsden in Sydney following their arrival. Later, when Ruatara's attempt to return to his hapu resulted in him being abandoned on Norfolk Island, again unpaid, by another unscrupulous sea captain, he stayed again with Marsden at his home in Parramatta.

Ruatara was a man of exceptional intelligence, an intelligence that prompted his desire to explore the white world, and even to seek its source in London, in a situation and at a time when visiting London was as fantastic as interplanetary travel is to us. In spite of his unfortunate experiences, he believed that there were benefits to be gained from white culture, especially from agricultural technology, and he sought to advance his knowledge of this wherever possible. Certainly the Reverend Samuel Marsden would have encouraged Ruatara, because he believed that conversion of the New Zealanders to Christianity would only be successful if British-European culture was imposed on them first, and their own social structure destroyed. Ruatara, on the other hand, saw in his plans for agricultural improvement the opportunity to increase the food supply and trading potential of his people, and as a result was particularly interested in those aspects of the proffered culture that would advance his cause.

By the time he finally left Sydney for home, Ruatara had been well briefed by Marsden on his plans for a missionary settlement in the Bay of Islands; for his part, Ruatara had agreed to help facilitate these, if only to advance his own mana by gaining the agricultural skills he considered advantageous. Perhaps he also thought that the presence of a few white settlers would help him adapt their agricultural practices to New Zealand conditions, and could help establish a regular trading link between the Ngapuhi of the Bay of Islands and the colony of New South Wales.

At the end of his five-year adventure, Ruatara returned to the Bay of Islands with the seed wheat and agricultural tools he believed he needed to begin his plan. Within a year he had planted and harvested wheat, much to the astonishment of most of his compatriots, and shortly after had ground it into flour and cooked a simple loaf, the first for each of these achievements in New Zealand. His promise to Marsden was fulfilled shortly afterwards, and the first missionaries began to build the first mission station on land granted by Ruatara next to his own pa at Rangihoua, north of the entrance to the Bay of Islands.

During his continued contact with Marsden, Ruatara maintained his demands for further agricultural implements and seeds with which to improve on the success he had had with wheat. For a man to whom European culture was absolutely unknown, his efforts at understanding and using aspects of it were remarkable. He was in many ways the original pioneer of modern New Zealand, and it is possible, even probable, that he also added an unexpected twist to the New Zealand rose story.

One of the persistent legends of New Zealand rose growing is that the first roses, specimens of Slater's Crimson China, were brought here

Rangihoua, home of horticultural pioneer and visionary Ngapuhi rangatira, Ruatara, who introduced wheat, European agriculture, missionaries and possibly roses to New Zealand. Was this where roses first bloomed in Aotearoa/New Zealand?
"Range Hue [sic] a New Zealand Fortified Village", Augustus Earl (Rex Nan Kivell Collection, National Library of Australia)

on the brig *Active*, when it transported the original missionary settlers to Rangihoua in 1814. There is no evidence of this at all, and no evidence in descriptions of the Rangihoua settlement that the little crimson rose was growing in the missionary gardens there — in spite of detailed reports by a number of visitors, and Marsden's own careful recording of his project. Nor do any of the lists of animals or plants brought to Rangihoua in the first years include roses. All we do have is a legend claiming Rangihoua as the source of the old Slater's Crimson Chinas that are to be found in the garden of Kemp House in Kerikeri.

If those roses did come from Rangihoua, how did they get there if not via the missionary settlers? Perhaps the luck of the rose played its hand when Ruatara was learning about agriculture on Marsden's farm at Parramatta. The portability of Slater's Crimson China, the fact that 'it may be reared in a coffee cup', made it easy to transport and popular in established British colonial settlements, especially those as distant from the delights of civilisation as Sydney. The garden plants that Sydney nurseries had available when Ruatara was seeking seed wheat and other agricultural supplies would have included small potted plants of this rose, plants that bloomed throughout the year with attractive crimson flowers, just the colour to catch the young rangatira's attention.

It is important to remember that Maori interest in white culture during the early years, not just that of Ruatara, was focused on those items that could enhance mana. For this reason, Hongi Hika was most interested in weapons that would give him greater strength in war; Ruatara was similarly attracted to agricultural technology, and greater strength in trade. Throughout New Zealand, white-owned vessels traded tools and weapons in exchange for the supplies and sexual favours they sought from the Maori: tools, weapons and anything red, for the Maori valued red above all other colours, a value heightened by its rarity in the plumage of local birds, and the brief season and delicacy of pohutukawa and rata blossom. Red wool and other red materials that could be used for decoration were an important item of trade for whalers and sealers working the New Zealand coast around 1800.

The red flowers of Slater's Crimson China, growing happily in its little pots, would have been a special treasure for Ruatara returning home on the *Ann* in 1812, for he had, in Marsden's words, 'laboured early and late to acquire useful knowledge, and particularly that of agriculture. ...and was fully convinced that the wealth and happiness of a nation depended much upon the produce of its soil.' We assume this statement referred to wheat and similar food items, but it would not be so exceptional for a visionary like Ruatara to see in this small, red rose further opportunities for wealth and happiness.

If Ruatara did bring the first roses amongst the new treasures in his luggage, neither their arrival nor fate are recorded. If they had been planted in display gardens, surely this would have been noted by the advance missionary team on its arrival early in 1814, or by the main body when it established itself later that year — but no such record remains. However, given the considerable value attributed to their red colour, and especially its association with rangatiratanga, it is likely that the roses would have been planted in a special place accessible only to the rangatira and his close associates. As Ruatara died within weeks of the mission's establishment, and the Rangihoua Pa and its community subsequently went into a rapid decline, ultimately to be abandoned, without Ruatara's special understanding the crimson rose and its mana would have been lost to the hapu.

Slater's Crimson China, sturdy little plant that it is, would have survived neglect. When the missionaries also abandoned Rangihoua in favour of more favourable locations at Kerikeri, Te Waimate and Paihia, they took with them whatever scrapings of white civilisation could be found; straggling China roses from the deserted pa could have been amongst these. If Kemp House's China roses did come from Rangihoua, this tale of vision, courage and luck is as suitable a beginning for the New Zealand rose mystery as any.

Ultimately it was Ruatara's uncle, Hongi Hika, who used white technology to realise his dream, a dream of conquest and slaughter, which has become the Ngapuhi legacy to New Zealand. The rose mystery, however, suggests that there is another legacy from this seminal period in New Zealand's history: Ruatara's dream of enhancing his mana with bountiful gardens, carefully tended to provide wealth and happiness for his people. It is a dream that has proven more reliable, and is symbolised as much as anything by the fragrant crimson roses that bloom in front of the old mission house in Kerikeri, at the heart of what was once bloody Hongi's domain.

The first 40 years of the nineteenth century were the missionary years, when settlements were established by evangelical adventurers as cultural bridgeheads for their faith, and were permitted by various tribes who saw the stations as a means for arming themselves. Overwhelmingly outnumbered by Maori, who considered that the settlers were their property, the missionary 'mechanics' walled their homes and gardens in behind high fences and hedges. It is not surprising that the rose most frequently mentioned in descriptions of New Zealand during this period is Sweet Briar.

With its pretty, subtle pink flower and fresh apple fragrance, Sweet Briar is the Eglantine of old England's hedgerows and Shakespearian verse. As the Church Missionary Society men and women fought to

The pre-Raphaelite painters of Victorian Britain worked on many of the most romantic themes from English literature, and in this scene from Shakespeare's *Hamlet*, drowned Ophelia drifts down a very English stream, the banks overgrown and touched with the white of Sweetbriar, the wild rose of chastity.

The pre-Raphaelites reworked many of the allegories from Classic times, not least the rose, into the popular romanticism of nineteenth-century Britain, and subsequently New Zealand, where they were no less popular.

"Ophelia", John Everett Millais (By courtesy of the Tate Gallery, London)

ABOVE: An important figure to Victorian Britain's Romantics, Chatterton was an immensely talented young poet who made the grand romantic gesture of committing suicide. With heavy symbolism typical of the time, a rose is painted in, signifying sorrow, sacrifice, death and transient talent. In its little pot, it appears to be Crimson China, the traveller that made it to New Zealand in body, and, it seems, in spirit.

"Chatterton", Henry Wallis (Courtesy of the Tate Gallery, London)

OPPOSITE: Perhaps the greatest of the Dutch flower painters, van Huijsum captures in this finely detailed painting the glory of Dutch floriculture that continues today. Not least of the lush blooms in this painting are the wonderfully baroque centifolias (lower right), the first of the modern, purpose-bred roses.

"Flowers in a terracotta vase", Jan van Huijsum (Reproduced by courtesy of the Trustees, The National Gallery, London)

The pre-eminent New Zealand painter for over fifty years, Frances Hodgkins often dealt with gardening themes, sometimes realistically, as in this early work. Often in her later years that changed to a more 'inside-looking-out' view, one that frequently touched on some of the oldest garden allegories of fertility and abandon.

"Gardening", Frances Hodgkins

establish their outposts of English propriety amidst turbulent land-scapes and unruly people, this was as good a reminder of English calm as any plant. In addition, Sweet Briar's quick growth and tough springy branches fully armed with thorns made it the ideal plant with which to build an impenetrable hedge.

The earliest mention of roses in New Zealand was made by Marsden when he listed marigolds, lilac, carnations and roses as the flowers growing in Kerikeri in 1820. Considering the first house at Kerikeri, that to be occupied by Rev. John Butler, was not yet built, and the only construction completed was the fence, this does little to con-firm the presence of either Sweet Briar or Slater's Crimson China, or any other particular rose. However, Sweet Briar is mentioned by a number of later visitors as being established as a hedge in Paihia, Kerikeri and Te Waimate, three of the earliest mission stations, and also at what remained of the original site at Rangihoua in 1841.

In 1834, William Barret Marshall visited the Bay of Islands on two occasions on the British naval ship the *Alligator*. He wrote an attractive description of the Mission church at Paihia in October, when the Sweet Briar he described would have just been coming into flower.

> The chapel at Paihia is very neat, I had almost said beautiful. It stands back from the road in an enclosed square, within the fence on all sides of which the sweet brier [sic] forms an impervious hedge, and mixes its perfume with the breeze, thus scenting the pure atmosphere breathed by those who assemble on this spot to worship God.

A pretty scene, but the fence and rose hedge illustrate further the some-what besieged state of the mission settlements, an observation made ten years earlier by an ensign on the French ship *Coquille* when writing of Rangihoua: 'The houses of Messrs Hall and King are a short distance from the beach. The courtyards and gardens which surround them are pallisaded...and surrounded by a [2.5-metre] wall and solid gate.'

It was up to the Rev. Richard Taylor, writing in 1841, to provide

Rangihoua a little of the charm hindsight affords, noting that roses had a place at the first mission station when he said of the by-then deserted scene, '…a few sweet briar bushes are the tokens of it once having been the abode of civilised man.'

Darwin said there were 'whole hedges of sweet briar' at Paihia, which he saw in 1835 during the New Zealand section of his famous voyage on the *Beagle*; and Waimate also had Sweet Briar hedges, which attracted comment from a number of visitors over the years. Darwin also wrote, somewhat loosely for a scientific observer, of 'roses of several kinds' at Paihia, and 'many different kinds of flowers' at Waimate, suggesting that roses were more than hedges in the English enclaves the missionaries had created, a fact confirmed by the trader Joel Samuel Polack.

Polack ran a trading store at Kororareka from 1833 to 1841, and in 1838 published a book on his New Zealand experiences, *New Zealand; Being a Narrative of Travels and Adventures*. In this he made the first published comments on the cultivation of roses in New Zealand, indicating early on the success that was possible, and confirmed the establishment of at least Sweet Briar and China roses by 1837: 'Thus the graveolent sweet briar, China, and other roses…become with trifling care, perfectly acclimatised to the soil.'

In the early years of the missionary period it was exceedingly hard for the 'mechanics' employed by Marsden to tempt the Maori with the benefits of European culture. While reading and writing, and the artisan skills of carpentry, milling, smithing and the like, had some appeal, and advanced farming or horticulture were a very attractive proposition, most Maori saw the missionaries as a means of bolstering their fighting strength with modern arms, and allowed the settlements to survive only so long as they continued to supply the arms and equipment the Maori required. In 1829 it is estimated there were less than 120 Europeans living in the Bay of Islands; the settlers' survival rested entirely with their Maori hosts, who generally treated the missionaries and their settlements as possessions of the hapu under whose authority they sur-

vived. It was not unusual for their gardens, stores, even homes, to be raided at will, especially when a taua was preparing for a raid.

As well as living in such unpredictable circumstances, the hardship of limited and irregular supplies demanded that settlement gardens provide as much food as possible, and there was little space, or time, to spend on elaborate flower beds. Sweet Briar and the China roses were suited to this situation; indeed, they probably both made their way to New Zealand in this early period simply because they were hardy plants, and, in the case of Sweet Briar, because it was so well suited to doing good service as a hedge.

The people who volunteered to suffer such extreme conditions in the cause of evangelism were not the types who followed closely the fashions of home, and the conditions they laboured under when they reached this isolated and savage corner of the world did nothing to encourage any belated gestures in this area. It was enough that the roses they had reminded them of home and of a hoped-for civilisation to come, and that they were hardy enough to survive neglect when more important gardening matters pressed. Indeed, the fact that roses were brought at all is an indication of how fundamental the rose image was, and that they survived, how resilient the rose mystery.

By the time Polack's book was published the missionary period was drawing to a close and New Zealand was entering its colonial phase. At the 15 mission sites that had been established around the country, Sweet Briar and the China roses were common. Mrs Selwyn's description of her return to Waimate in 1844 to 'an Arch of Flowers under wh. we passed, chiefly China roses' is a sign of just how much the flowers of Slater's Crimson China, and possibly even Parson's Pink China, were an important component of the mission gardens in this period.

There is evidence of other roses too, indicating that there were those amongst the missionaries who placed importance on gardens producing beauty as well as food. One of these was George Clarke, the schoolmaster who moved into the mission house at Kerikeri in 1827. One of his children, George junior, recorded in his *Notes on an Early Life in New Zealand* that his father had '...got a box of plants from Sydney, among them some precious cabbage Roses the first I suppose that were grown in New Zealand.' Clarke wrote this 75 years after the event, so it may not be as accurate as a contemporary record; however, it is the first indication of the presence of either Centifolia or Moss roses (depending on what the ten-year-old George Clarke called cabbage roses) in New Zealand.

Polack certainly implies that there were other roses in the northern area by 1837, and it is possible that his fellow traders in the Bay of Islands, James Clendon and Gilbert Mair, were instrumental in their

McDonnell established a formal garden around his home, overlooking the shipyard that he had recently purchased, and he bought a gardener over from London to oversee it. That man, John Edgerley, lived in this cottage on the shore beneath McDonnell's homestead and became an important figure in colonial gardening in New Zealand. He regularly traded with the Royal Gardens at Kew, imported plants in Wardian cases from London, and sent samples of New Zealand flora in return. In 1842, ten varieties of rose were sent to Thomas McDonnell from Kew, although there is no record of exactly what they were. In 1843, five roses were sent to Edgerley, plus *R. banksii* (sic), after he had left the employ of McDonnell, with the intention of setting up a nursery business in Auckland. No doubt these were the "few good roses, white moss if you can spare it," that Edgerley had requested from Kew by letter in November 1842.

"McDonnell House", John Kinder (Auckland City Art Gallery)

introduction. With the boom in whaling around the New Zealand coast during the 1830s, the Bay of Islands became a very busy port. As many as ten whaling ships a month would visit for supplies and recreation, as would other vessels such as sealers and timber ships. Such activity attracted traders, whose business produced enough wealth and stability for them to establish homes and, for those with families like the Mairs or pretensions like the Clendons, homes with gardens; gardens with roses.

Elizabeth and Gilbert Mair, a retired Scots sea captain, established a trading station on the Te Wahapu peninsula in 1830. Next to the station they built themselves a home with a spacious garden, which was likely to have contained roses. Given the access the Mairs had to the nurseries and plant dealers in Sydney through their trade contacts, it seems likely that this garden became the site of many rose introductions over the following years.

Unfortunately there is no direct evidence of this, other than the general references of visitors such as Darwin to the roses in Paihia, and a lingering reputation that the Mair garden was one of the finest in the Bay of Islands. Mair's competitor, James Clendon, had a house at Okiato which also had a garden, but it seems to have been less well kept than the Mairs' and was described in 1840 by Mrs Felton Mathew as having 'a few rose trees and geraniums, but all very much neglected.'

The gardens of the Mairs and the Clendons, and that of another trader, Thomas McDonnell at Horeke on the Hokianga Harbour, were the harbingers of the next stage in the New Zealand rose story. By this time the real pioneer roses of New Zealand, Sweet Briar and Crimson China, had served their purpose. They would be totally displaced within 20 years of the signing of the Treaty of Waitangi, first by the real garden roses of old England and then by the next generation of hybrid marvels. The hardiness of China and Sweet Briar was the essence of their success, and of their survival, and they can still be found in many parts of what could be called 'old' New Zealand, as pretty a link with our roots as a nation as any.

5 Taking the land

The jasmine flower is English rhyme,
The rose is an English tale.
But censered from the open hills,
The native tang comes drifting in
Prayer of two worlds my garden fills;
Born of two worlds I watch a third begin.

The Old Homestead, *Alan Mulgan*

New Zealand became established in the years after 1840, changing from a frontier place, wild with adventure and danger, into a new colony. British rule brought order, formality and a feeling of inclusion to the settlers, a feeling that attracted new immigrants planning not just to profit from the opportunities available in a new colony but to settle and to make themselves a new home. The white presence was no longer reliant on Maori support and fashioned entirely for survival; it had become, in attitude at least, self-sufficient and intent on coercion of the whole country to European values. As readily transferable symbols of those values, gardens and especially roses were immediately put to the task of creating little bits of Britain at the edges of New Zealand's bush, bits that flourished and grew as fast as the new colony.

The missionary roses of the frontier years became obsolete as garden roses almost as soon as British sovereignty was proclaimed, and the Governor had settled into his official residence at Okiato. Hard times at the outer edge of Empire were suitable for hardy, weed-like roses such as Crimson China, which could grow almost anywhere with or without attention. Sweet Briar similarly was a hardy survivor, one with the considerable advantage of being an excellent, virile hedge plant, well equipped with savage thorns to keep un-invited visitors and beasts at bay. They were not, however, glamorous plants that graced elegant gardens, not the sort of thing the colony's first official surveyor, Felton Mathew, recommended in 1841 in a letter to Governor Hobson: 'There is a great want of fine flowers in New Zealand, and every introduction of that kind improves the landscape.'

New Zealand's overwhelming greenness must have caused many new residents to yearn for a glimmer of red, just as Ruatara may have done, and tiny pockets of 'improvement' had already begun during the 1830s. The gardens of successful businessmen Gilbert Mair, James Clendon and Thomas McDonnell represented the positions their owners considered appropriate for men of wealth. In the Hokianga, the fortune McDonnell had accumulated by 1835 allowed him to pursue his interest in botany by bringing to his Horeke home a gardener, John Edgerley, probably the first specialist gardener employed in New Zealand. McDonnell and Edgerley collected botanic specimens from the Northland bush to send to collectors in Europe, and brought to New Zealand a number of exotic plants. One of these is reputed to be the now widespread Norfolk Pine, as well as examples of various gums and other Australian species, and fruit trees. It is likely that they also brought roses from New South Wales, or perhaps even from China where McDonnell had served in the opium trade, to decorate the McDonnell gardens, which according to the missionary James Buller were of 'rare pretension'.

An exploration of the site of McDonnell's house, which burned down in 1842, in the spring of 1993 revealed three roses pushing their way through clumps of grass, survivors of years of grazing and neglect. They were the small, very early rambler Laure Davoust, which would have been brand new in 1842, and *R. laevigata*, the gracious white rose known as the Cherokee Rose, and the ubiquitous colonial Sweet Briar. All were growing at the edge of that pretentious garden, now a battered

Général Jacqueminot
Vivian Ward

piece of paddock with a bedraggled clutch of surviving plants from what was once a fine collection of horticultural exotica.

The commerce that had produced such garden outposts as Mair's and McDonnell's was a singularly northern phenomenon prior to 1840. Other than the scattered whaling and sealing stations around the country further south, there were no permanent European settlements at all in New Zealand before then and it was only in the Bay of Islands and the Hokianga that substantial trading was possible and profitable enough to permit the luxury of such gardens. The change after 1840, however, was dramatic, and as the white population of New Zealand exploded from less than 1000 in 1840 to more than 30,000 by 1855, so too did commercial opportunities and European cultural activity. Making New Zealand like home was the predominant intention of most settlers, and while pianos, paintings and books were shipped around the world to meet the need for culture, it was gardening that satisfied the demand most quickly and completely.

The settlers' gardens were initially more like those of the missionaries than the gardens of their plans. They needed to grow food before anything else, and vegetable plants and seeds were often essential for survival in the first few years. Hedges were also important, and the demand for Sweet Briar, although already well established in many coastal settlements, was enough for its seed to continue to be imported for a number of years. Other roses also found their way into the new gardens, however, and not just hardy Crimson Chinas but the pretty blooms of old Britain.

To most of the immigrants, 'home' was Britain, where the hedge rose and garden rose were well entrenched, where rose plants and rose images were being promoted in every sphere of fashion. In the arts, romanticism had again shaken the dust off the rose mystery with poems rich in rose allegory and novels that evoked the ancient powers of Mother Nature, the Great Goddess herself. By mid-Victorian times, the pre-Raphaelites were enlivening things with their precisely painted medieval morality tales, which had a richness of rose symbolism unseen in painting since the Renaissance. Even for those who had no direct contact with the countryside, or gardens, before they embarked for New Zealand, the garden and the rose were as familiar as any symbol from their mother culture.

At the same time, gardening flourished as botanists introduced more and more possibilities from worldwide expeditions and continual experimentation with hybridising. The popularity of botany had spread throughout the British middle class, and gardening as well as plant collecting thrived through various periodicals, societies and regular competitions seeking perfect examples of fruit and flower. Roses benefited from this surge of interest as, against the trend for the exotic, it was the established varieties that became an integral part of the popularly conceived English 'cottage' garden, fashionable in Britain at the time. It was these roses that replaced the Chinas and Sweet Briar in the first years of colonial New Zealand.

France was the centre of rose innovation during Victorian times, a fact highlighted by Mrs Catherine Gore's influential rose book, *The Rose Fanciers' Manual*, published in 1838. She wrote the book, she says in the preface, '...to render every amateur a rose-grower' and to attract them to the advantages of France's new rose families, which she considered to be seriously neglected in England in spite of their charms. As an observer of British gardening at the time, her criticism is an interesting assessment of the state of British rose breeding on the eve of New Zealand's establishment period. She wrote:

> It is universally admitted that since the establishment of the Horticultural Society, the art of gardening has made greater progress in England than in any European country. In a few specific branches, and more particularly in the culture of roses, France, however, still maintains the pre-eminence; and while receiving from England her finest specimens of the dahlia, sends us in return an annual importation of roses, standards, and even stocks for grafting... The French believe that the English have the best roses in the

world...[but] in England a new rose remains for years a rarity...although the beautiful novelties of France...may be purchased for about the value of sixpence.

Settlers of the first organised settlements in New Zealand arrived within three years of the publication of this book, at Wellington and New Plymouth. Whatever the difficulties of the next few years, as the settlements grew in spite of disillusionment, disputes with the Maori over land ownership, and a shortage of materials and services, those first settlers' intentions had been set by the time Mrs Gore's book had changed attitudes in Britain. The roses they intended to plant in their new gardens, even if it took some time before they could get around to it, would be those of the cottage or farm gardens of England, which, according to Mrs Gore, 'adhere almost exclusively to the Cabbage Rose, Damask, and Maiden's Blush.'

Around the young colony, far away from the Bay of Islands and Hokianga, gardens Mrs Gore would have recognised as members of the English farm garden family were being established. A brief resident of New Zealand during the 1850s, while her husband was busy founding Christchurch, Charlotte Godley frequently commented on the settlers' gardens in letters to her mother at home, and it seems she often encountered roses that would have confirmed Mrs Gore's opinions. During a stay in the rather tatty young settlement of Wellington in 1850, she wrote to her mother in February, shortly after her arrival: 'The garden is really very pretty, only a little out of order, with sweetbriar, honeysuckle, clove pinks, and white moss roses, and other real English plants scarcely yet out of flower.' The 'English' plants seemed to be quite a comfort to her, as was the fact that the house and garden were well protected by a fence, on account of the disturbingly wild-looking Maori she had seen and met (and some less than respectable Europeans).

Mrs Godley moved on to Canterbury less than a year after her arrival in Wellington, but not before she noted that the roses of the town, with the exception of Sweet Briar, did not seem to do very well.

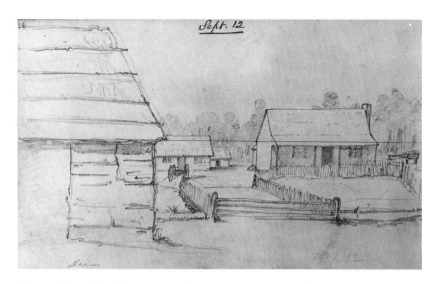

Home of the earliest European gardening pioneers in Canterbury, Deans House, Riccarton, was a haven of English gentility for travellers from Lyttelton. While there is no record of roses in the garden, it is possible that they were grown here.
"Deans House, Riccarton", Walter Mantell (Alexander Turnbull Library)

This does not seem surprising for the time of year — August — and is at some odds with her comments a few months later in November, when she writes: 'The flowers were beautiful, roses of all kinds in perfection.' In Canterbury, where Christchurch was still just a plan, there were few examples of roses for her to write about, so she set about planting the cuttings that had been supplied to her by friends in Wellington, noting shortly after, '…the little bits of sweetbriar that were sent to me some months ago from Wellington were positively sweet, and full of leaf, and so were the rose trees. We do not aspire to flowers for this year.'

These gifts from Wellington would soon be supplemented by eleven new roses sent out from the Royal Gardens at Kew to Edward Jerningham Wakefield at the Canterbury settlement in 1851, a collection that included the classics Souvenir de Malmaison (sic), and Baronne Prevost, as well as the China rose, Cramoisie Superieur (sic). Also included were Red China, Bougere, Dombowski, Duchess of Sutherland, Leopold de Bauffremont, Madame Dameme, and Renife d'Ormond, all of which seem to have vanished from the records, although Red China is possibly Slater's Cromson China, or even the original China Rose that was last recorded in China in 1885, but this seems unlikely.

Unfortunately she never did write to say whether she received any of these for her own garden, as seems probable, or if her Wellington cuttings did flower the following year, but her reference to the Sweet Briar cutings serves to highlight this invaluable means of distributing flowers and other plants that the settlers used throughout New Zealand, something that remains a feature of gardening in New Zealand today. It was probably through cuttings that roses like Slater's Crimson China, Parson's Pink China and Sweet Briar were spread around New Zealand during the missionary period, which may cast some light on why Parson's Pink is known in some parts of the country as The Bishop's Rose. Some legends tell of the Catholic Bishop Pompallier prompting this name by his distribution of cuttings of this, his favourite rose, around the country when visiting various and of the China roses found in Akaroa, where the French settler community were frequent hosts of the Bishop.

The small Banks Peninsula town of Akaroa and its surrounding countryside were settled in 1840 by a tiny group of 63 French colonists. The only French settlement in the country, it became the source of the many references to roses and other aspects of French character that have ever since been attributed to Banks Peninsula. The origins of the legend of French roses being brought to Akaroa by the settlers, however, seem rather elusive; the 'old' roses frequently celebrated as part of the French connection, such as Slater's Crimson China, and even the Bishop's own Parson's Pink, are more likely to have come from other settlements, where their presence was recorded earlier, than to have been brought out from France.

Charlotte Godley's 1851 description of the garden of Akaroa's resident magistrate seems to indicate that the village's roses at that time were similar to, if not the same as, the old English favourites common elsewhere: 'You go through a very neat gate up a nicely kept little path of lawn, a beautiful stream on one side, and on the other a high hedge of roses, the monthly ones in full blow, and the cabbage, provence, etc, just beginning.'

Reflecting on Mrs Gore's comments about the French rose-growing fashions of 1838, it is even less likely that these roses came from France in 1840. If the settlers had brought roses with them, it is probable that they would have been representatives of one of the new rose families that were immensely popular in French gardens in 1839, which went on to set standards of rose form and character throughout the rose growing world. Rather than being French in character, the famous old roses of Akaroa are the epitome of British tradition, the sort of thing to be found around a Surrey cottage rather than a Lyon garden.

However, French rose breeding talent and promotional energy, with help from Mrs Gore, was about to change the British predilection for conservative rose growing. It was also to have a profound influence on New Zealand gardens once settlements had been consolidated into towns, and order and commerce had been established. Over the next 150 years, French rose breeders would give New Zealand many of their most famous roses, and in the second half of the nineteenth century the avalanche of new varieties the French produced gave growers in the colony a rich choice from which to develop their own rose traditions.

Undoubtedly French rose breeders led the world by 1850, after a remarkable half-century of creativity and industry. This was made possible by French enthusiasm for roses and for new roses in particular, an enthusiasm that was a consequence of the remarkable rose-growing passion of the Empress Josephine. As the wife of Europe's most powerful leader, Napoleon Bonaparte, Josephine's wealth and influence were enormous, giving her the ability to draw on resources from across the continent and almost every corner of the globe, and for her activities to have an equally widespread impact. At her country estate, 'La Malmaison', Josephine spent a small fortune on landscaping and rose plants, and through the services of the leading rosarians and gardeners of the time created a rose garden of startling proportions, a garden that stimulated great interest in roses amongst professional and amateur gardeners throughout France and, ultimately, throughout the world.

The orderly, fertile, well-tended settlement that Mrs Godley visited is apparent
from this later view. It is not surprising that the peninsula is famed for its old roses,
for in such a cultivated environment they would have prospered.
"Akaroa, 1866", W. M. N. Watkins (Rex Nan Kivell Collection, Australian National Gallery)

It is one of the rose mystery's greatest coups that roses should be
the particular delight of such a powerful person as the Empress of
France. During the period in which Josephine collected and planted her
roses, Napoleonic France was the centre of the greatest European
empire since Roman times; the garden at La Malmaison became as influential in the cultivation of roses as the famous gardens at Paestum
had been in the time of ancient Rome. La Malmaison was exemplary in
a number of ways, all of them fashionable because of their association
with Josephine. Simply by having a huge rose collection, rose gardens
were accepted as being suitable for grand estates, while the variety of
types and species served to illustrate just how adaptable roses were to a
range of garden situations. These alone were important advances which
endorsed the value of Josephine's work, but she made her greatest
impression on the development of new roses, a process that benefited
immensely from the huge and varied collection she amassed at La
Malmaison, and the talent she also collected to facilitate her plans.

To create La Malmaison, the Empress acquired the services of the best gardening minds of Europe. Three of these were to prove outstanding contributors, who ultimately ensured the experiment of Josephine's garden continued well after the fall of the garden itself. Naturally, the pre-eminent French rose specialist of the day, André Dupont, was approached early. He was a brilliant rose hybridist and creative gardener who is credited with inventing the standard rose bush. He was also responsible for the superb rose collection at the Luxembourg Gardens in Paris. Seconded too were France's leading botanist, Jacques-Martin Cels, from the Institute National de France, and the remarkable English rosarian, John Kennedy.

Seeking Kennedy's assistance was an incredible cheek, even for Josephine. In spite of his reputation as Europe's leading rose grower, and the advantages to be gained from the experience of the London firm of Lee and Kennedy of which he was a principal, France was fighting a bitter war with the United Kingdom and the Royal Navy had a tight blockade on French ports. It shows how adamant Josephine's plans for La Malmaison were that he was approached at all, and the subsequent involvement of Kennedy, including his travel between the warring countries with examples of his own experiments and cuttings of new roses for the gardens is a fantastic episode in the rose mystery.

This peculiar subterfuge could not have happened without support on both sides of the Channel. As well as Josephine's intervention with the French military and border officials, the knowledge and discreet support of the British Government, and especially of the Prime Minister, the 3rd Duke of Portland, was essential. It seems appropriate that such an episode should bring about the creation of a new rose family, romantic that it should carry the name of one of the protagonists. During one of his clandestine trips to Paris, it seems that Kennedy secured a rare dark-pink version of the miniature Autumn Damask known in France as Le Petit Quatre Saisons, which he took back with him to England and successfully crossed with Slater's Crimson China. The resulting rose became known, in Britain and in France, as the

Duchess of Portland rose, no doubt in honour of the Prime Minister's wife. The family it started, the Portland roses, were for a number of years the hottest roses in France.

Portland roses became a favourite with the cultivists who were busy breeding new types to satisfy the voracious French appetite for new roses, which had been aroused by the fascinating collection of ancient and bizarre examples at La Malmaison. By the time of Josephine's death in 1814, La Malmaison contained the largest collection of roses yet assembled, with more than 250 varieties, including 22 of the new Chinas, 27 Centifolias, three Mosses, one Musk rose, nine Damasks, one of the very rare and ancient family, *Hulthemia persica*, and no less than 167 Gallicas. While the rose garden quickly dissipated after Josephine died, and few roses, if any, were still in the garden by the end of Waterloo year, the Portlands and other new roses that La Malmasion fostered completely changed the image and substance of roses forever.

Josephine brought about a French dominance of rose breeding that was almost total, and France became the destination for exotic roses collected or bred in every corner of the globe. As new species arrived from Asia, they were seized with as much relish by French breeders as were the new creations of breeders from other countries almost as soon as they bloomed. These became raw materials for a succession of new roses, some briefly fashionable, others that had the garden presence to last, and some that are still considered classics. New and glamorous in the late Victorian age, these were the roses of young colonial New Zealand, the cultivated jewels of colour used to embellish its wild and rampant green.

One of the first French offerings originated in America, the work of one John Champney, which was shaped and sent from Paris as the first Noisette. A cross between one of the new Asian roses, Parson's Pink China, and the old Musk rose, *R. moschata*, the original, known as Champney's Pink Cluster, attracted the attention of an immigrant cultivist who had a nursery in Charleston, Phillipe Noisette. He sent examples to his Parisian brother, Louis, who crossed it with another of the new Asians, Park's Yellow Tea-Scented Rose, and produced the first of the rose family that brought yellow into colonial New Zealand gardens. Noisette yellow was a stronger and more resilient colour than previous rose yellows and it secured a regular, if small, place in the catalogues of colonial nurseries, even those that did not specialise in roses.

The yellow Noisette climber, Cloth of Gold, produced in the Coquereau nursery in 1843, was considered one of the finest roses in New Zealand, and was available at least as early as 1860 from nurseries in both Auckland and Nelson, where it fetched a premium of 4/- a plant, four times that charged for a *Banksia* climber. Cloth of Gold became a classic, a rose which author Nancy Steen found in 'Quite a few of our oldest gardens and settlements, all over the country...' when exploring in search of old roses. It was still being recommended as a climber suitable for New Zealand gardens in 1920, by which time fashion had completely overlooked the rest of the Noisette family.

If Noisettes were very much an interesting diversion, the arrival in France of another new variety, the Bourbons, was to have a greater influence on rose evolution. This rose was named after the beautiful island of Réunion, a French overseas department in the Indian Ocean, which was known at the time as the Ile de Bourbon. A French government botanist discovered a new rose on the island, which appeared to be a cross between Parson's Pink China and the Autumn Damask, which had played such an important part in the birth of Portlands at about the same time. Dutifully, the botanist, M Breon, sent seeds of this new rose back to France, where it immediately assumed the name Rose de l'Ile de Bourbon.

Like the Noisettes, the Bourbons as a family became an interesting and, for a time, popular attraction, but their greatest value was as an intermediary stage in the progress towards more advanced roses. In New Zealand they were available from the earliest nurseries, taking up the same proportion of colonial nursery catalogues as Noisettes and becoming similarly less important as more of the highly fashionable

Hybrid Perpetuals became available. Their presence has been a lasting one, however, and roses such as Souvenir de la Malmaison, Bourbon Queen, La Reine Victoria and Zephirine Drouhin form such an influential group of classic pinks that they could be called the archetypal old-fashioned roses of New Zealand.

The precious, delicate pink Souvenir de la Malmaison, one of the roses sent out to E. J. Wakefield in 1851, ironically on the ship *Duke of Portland*, appears in the 1860 catalogue of Nelson's pioneer nurseryman, William Hale, either as a survivor from that Kew Garden shipment, or from a later arrival. Baronne Prevoste was another Hale listing that was also in that Wardian case from Kew, perhaps the earliest known example of a Hybrid Perpetual in New Zealand. Along with La Reine Victoria and Bourbon Queen, also being offered by Hale in 1860, these were pinks to be reckoned with in the early years of antipodean rose growing, more so when they were joined by the last of the great Bourbons, Zephirine Drouhin, shortly after its release in France in 1868.

This fragrant company, all persistent flowerers, have thrived in New Zealand conditions for well over 100 years. In spite of a fancied notion that roses must be red, New Zealand gardeners have always shown a fondness for the gentle charm of pink roses, a reflection perhaps of a quest for soft beauty in a hard landscape. It is a quest which has survived any number of changes in fashion, and one which was well served by the accumulated delights of this fragrant, pink, delectably frilly Bourbon quartet and the new Hybrid Perpetual, a group which has enjoyed something of a revival as 'old-fashioned' roses have reclaimed a share of fashion.

Back in France the pace was really hotting up. The French people were wealthier than they had ever been before, and the half-century of peace that followed Napoleon's fall was a golden age of gardening, of rose gardening in particular. To meet increased demand, and the French predilection for fashion, cultivists and breeders worked frantically to create roses with new forms and colours, which if they found favour could make a fortune for the lucky breeder. Many new nurseries were established during this boom period, especially in the Lyon region. As a result, French culturists continued to dominate rose breeding throughout New Zealand's colonial period, and consequently the roses planted in New Zealand colonial gardens.

From the heat of competition came Hybrid Perpetuals, a blend of different Chinas with varying proportions of Bourbons and/or Portlands; a mix of the exotic and the traditional. Hybrid Perpetuals, another French creation, are as old as New Zealand, making their first appearance in Europe about the time of the Treaty of Waitangi in 1840. They soon made their way to New Zealand, where they received an enthusiastic welcome.

Compared to the other new rose families, and particularly to the old European roses, the Hybrid Perpetual family was sensationally prolific; the famous French garden of l'Hay-les-Roses claimed a collection of some 1700 varieties by the turn of the century. This dwarfed anything the rose world had known previously, and sheer weight of numbers could explain the preponderance of Hybrid Perpetuals offered in New

As one of New Zealand's planned colonies, the bareness of the streets and sparse gardens of New Plymouth are typical of the early colonial period. It was not yet a time for gardening on a grand scale, or even making a serious attempt at a cottage garden.
"The Town of New Plymouth, 1843", Emma Wickstead (Alexander Turnbull Library)

Zealand, alongside the other French inventions, Bourbons, Portlands and Noisettes, and remnants of the traditional roses of old England.

The French rose invasion also happened in Britain, perhaps as a consequence of Mrs Gore's efforts, and the popularity of Hybrid Perpetuals and their compatriots at 'home' would have been brought to the colony by the increasing numbers of settlers during the 1850s, '60s, and '70s. As towns and commerce became established, however, more of the supplies needed by new arrivals were available locally, and nursery businesses were able to provide their own lists of plants for new gardens as well as information pertinent to growing in local conditions. Those lists were predominantly of fruit trees and vegetable plants, but the urban sections that have always been a feature of New Zealand soon demanded garden plants of beauty and grace, as did the properties of speculators who planned to develop and sell quickly. The fashionable rose provided a quick and easy solution for both.

In spite of its British origins, the new colony did not always follow British patterns and there is evidence that a quite distinct colonial culture was developed partly out of a rejection of the British establishment. Aspects of this can be seen in the popularity of French roses, and in the assimilation of exotic tree species such as blue gums, Norfolk pines and macrocarpa, rather than oaks and elms. However, botanic experimentation was also fashionable in Britain at the time. Both Mair and McDonnell had Norfolk pines growing in their Northland gardens, and McDonnell was one of the first settlers to show an interest in cultivating exotics, as well as collecting and sending natives overseas.

Kew records show that roses were sent to McDonnell at least once, in 1842, when ten varieties of rose were included in a shipment of two Wardian boxes. It was requested that McDonnell return these boxes filled with different New Zealand plants from those already sent from previous collecting expeditions he had undertaken. It appears that McDonnell and Edgerley had been providing Kew and other English botanic collections with plants this way since at least 1836, shortly after Edgerley's arrival in the Hokianga.

McDonnell's trade during the 1830s and 1840s could hold the answer to a particular part of the rose mystery that has emerged in Taranaki. New Plymouth was one of the first settlements of the colonial period, and its garden traditions are some of the strongest in New Zealand, enhanced by the recent emergence of Egmont Nurseries as a leading rose grower and breeder. Most roses growing in the district during the establishment period were traditional English types of the intermediary stage between missionary utility Briars and Chinas and fashionable Hybrid Perpetuals and Noisettes, but a letter home from a New Plymouth settler in 1854 suggests that roses could have been arriving in New Zealand from sources other than nurseries in Australia, Britain or France.

Benjamin Wells was a leading figure in early New Plymouth, a lay preacher who would become editor of the local newspaper, and, as his regular correspondence to his mother in England reveals, an interested flower gardener. When he wrote describing his garden in 1854, he made particular reference to the roses, and amongst the expected Cabbages and Mosses he notes a couple of names that should have been unusual in Taranaki so soon after European settlement began. 'The following are now blooming and growing in our garden', he wrote. '…White Moss Rose, Cabbage Rose, Monthly Rose, Indica Minor Rose, Sanguinea Rose.'

Indica Minor is probably another of the China roses, which were frequently called 'indica' in Britain; in this case *R. chinensis minima*, sometimes called simply Minima or Miss Lawrence's Rose. In spite of the fact that this is not a rose with any traditional place in old New Zealand gardens, it was mentioned in Curtis's *Botanical Magazine* in 1815, and is the most logical candidate for this name.

Sanguinea Rose is another story. Sanguinea is a deep red China rose, which according to British rose historians was discovered in China in 1887. That is 33 years *after* Benjamin Wells wrote his letter, when the rose was flowering in his garden, and if this is the same rose, then it must have somehow found its way to New Zealand from China, rather than from Britain. If this is the case, and there is no evidence to either confirm or deny it, perhaps there is a link between Sanguinea and McDonnell, who had contacts with China, or with the troops who came to New Zealand directly from China.

Sanguinea is a nice piece of the rose mystery with which to end the first period of planned settlement in New Zealand. By 1860 a new influence was affecting rose growers: local nurseries. These small businesses quickly replaced the Sydney nurseries, which had supplied plants to the first colonists and were especially the source of roses for any gardener with pretensions. By the late 1850s, Sydney and Melbourne supplied many of the exciting new varieties — the Noisettes, Portlands and Hybrid Perpetuals — but New Zealand's own nurseries were already making roses much more accessible as they set up to supply the need for fruit trees and hedges, then gradually met the demand for roses as it came with establishment.

Miss Lawrence's Rose is probably the Indica Minor Rose that Benjamin Wells wrote of in 1854. (*Curtis' Botanical Magazine*, Rare Books Room, Auckland Central City Library)

Etoile de Holland
Vivian Ward

6 Midwives

As for the roses, you could not help feeling that they understood that roses are the only flowers that impress people at garden-parties; the only flowers that everybody is certain of knowing. Hundreds, yes, literally hundreds, had come out in a single night; the green bushes bowed down as though they had been visited by archangels.

The Garden Party, Katherine Mansfield

Roses suited colonial New Zealand. Their garish pretension fitted neatly into a society that presumed itself so special, so ordered, when other colonies were dishevelled, so polite when they were loud, and yet so vigorously new. They were also an important part of that most revered New Zealand institution, the garden.

From the time the first settlers built here, New Zealanders have had land around their houses — land they use to make their lot their home: growing food and providing protection, and creating the sanctity of a garden. While the journey from colony to dominion in 1907 included bitter depression as well as wild prosperity, and conditions were never quite as egalitarian as subsequent generations have been inclined to believe, the home garden was one of the few advantages of the new country that was almost universal.

Early on, these gardens were built inside protective fences or hedges in much the same way as medieval Europeans built their gardens within walls, and 'home' was everything within those walls. The extension of home into garden is a characteristic that remains from the early days of settlement, when the entrance to the home was not the front door but a front gate: open to public view, the garden as much as the house reflected the character of those who lived there. The high status of gardens in New Zealand dates from those times, as does the popularity of roses. It was the demand for rose plants from the many ordinary settlers who came to the colony that led the first nursery businesses to feature roses amongst their offerings.

Those first nurseries were established within months of the creation of the colony, and by 1843 there were at least three offering plants to settlers. In Wellington, James McBeth was selling plants and trees almost as soon as the New Zealand Company settlers landed; in Auckland, D. F. Carnegie was operating from Epsom, as was John Edgerley, who had left Horeke in 1842 when McDonnell's house burned down. McBeth, Carnegie and Edgerley specialised in the fruit tress that were in such demand, but both McBeth and Carnegie also offered a limited selection of flowering plants amongst their respective ranges of vegetables. Carnegie actually offered 'a few roses', though he did not specify what they were, and noted that his trees were 'superior to imported trees not having suffered from a long voyage.'

In promoting the benefits of his locally grown trees, Carnegie was competing with the offerings of traders and nurseries in New South Wales and Victoria. Lists from Australian nurseries were advertised in New Zealand and catalogues sent to settlers, creating tough competition for most local nurseries. This was especially so in the rose trade: the Australians had more extensive selections available, and had access to the latest creations from France. Competition also came from local merchants who brought in large consignments of plants and pre-sold them from published lists. Typical was an advertisement in the *Lyttleton Times* of 17 July 1851, which offered fruit trees, raspberries, strawberries, grape vines, roses and other flowering trees ex the *Torrington*.

The special consignment business did not last long, as nursery businesses became established in the various settlements around the coast, offering the same range of plants and trees as the merchants were able to secure but with the benefit, as Carnegie so clearly pointed out, of being New Zealand-grown. The lists of these local nurseries reflected the demands of the colony, which were predominantly for fruit trees and other useful plants such as grape and berry vines, as well as vegetables. Settlers needed sustenance first, and investment in productive land consumed all available capital and energy during the establishment years. Flowering plants, and especially expensive roses, were an adjunct to this mainstream business, and the range offered by most nurserymen was limited to the species and varieties already established, or extended to include only those traditional roses the settlers knew well from home. They had neither the time nor the energy to sell innovative new rose varieties to their customers.

Specialisation was avoided in most nurseries, although many plantsmen did have their preferences for particular areas of their business. Others acknowledged that certain plants had more prestige than others, and that roses in particular had an attraction that was good for their other business. Many made special references to roses in their advertisements, in the hope that this would enhance their reputation. Others, like David Hay in Auckland and Nelson's William Hale, expanded their rose selections enough to gain something of a reputation as rose specialists.

William Hale set up shortly after Nelson was established in 1841 and, because of the slow development of Nelson following the Wairau incident in 1843, actively marketed his plants in other colonial settlements such as Wellington, New Plymouth and Christchurch. Hay, however, essentially confined sales to the Auckland region, where he had created his Montpellier Nursery at the end of Seaview Road, Remuera, in 1855. Although he was a later arrival than Hale, Hay was soon considered one of the leading rose suppliers in the colony.

The markets each nursery serviced were essentially the same, and were divided into three areas, each of which required roses, if for slightly different purposes. The biggest market was the supply of home garden needs for permanent settlers; then there was the speculation market, which wanted quick-growing, attractive plants to rapidly

The Nurserymen's
Association, Annual
Conference. W. E. Lippiatt
is the third from the left in
the back row.

improve the value of their properties; finally there were the specialists, a small group of botanically literate gardeners and collectors who were always on the look out for exotics.

The colonial gardeners, who made up the biggest proportion of nursery business, were initially intent on establishing their homes and filling their gardens with fruit trees and other producing plants. They knew little about roses, other than wanting the beauty and style they offered for their gardens, and were happy to buy any rose so long as it was the appropriate colour. It is interesting to note that the traditional English roses included in William Hale's catalogue, roses like White Moss and Maiden's Blush, are absent from Hay's offerings at the same time. Hale's nursery predates Hay's by at least 12 years, and this particular difference between the two is a sign that the colony's gardeners quickly passed on from traditional varieties to the exciting offerings from France.

Part of the reason for this may lie in the character of those colonial nurserymen, and in the influence of the specialist botanists who were a small but extremely active group at the time. Acting as a figurehead for this group was undoubtedly Sir George Grey, Governor from 1845 to 1853, and again from 1861 to 1868, and for 20 years an MP in Auckland, including two years as Prime Minister to 1879. He was an enthusiastic botanist and arguably the greatest collector of plants in New Zealand, many of which were planted in the extensive grounds at his home, Mansion House on Kawau Island. As a patron of various horticultural and botanical activities in the colony he encouraged diverse gardening practices, and stimulated the experimental work of New Zealand's nurserymen.

Enthusiasm for experimentation and the challenge of exotics seems to have spread quickly into the area of rose growing in New Zealand. The new varieties being turned out by French breeders were at the leading edge of hybridisation, and they also had the advantage of being sound economic prospects for nurseries. Their elegant shapes and attractive colours were easily sold to gardeners who were not especially interested in botanical niceties, and who simply wanted beauty for their gardens.

George Grey was interested in the newest rose varieties himself, and through his regular trade with Kew Gardens in Britain, to whom he sent various New Zealand plants, especially ferns, he received rose specimens sent with other additions to his collection. Plants at the time were sent across the world in Wardian cases, mini glasshouses that kept the plants alive throughout their voyage. In 1863, a case sent to Grey by W. J. Hooker from Kew included three roses, unfortunately not named in the accompanying list, but unlikely to be something available from Grey's good friend, David Hay of Montpellier Nursery.

In 1861, while Grey was Governor, roses were ordered from William Hale for the Domain and Government House in Auckland. Although this is not necessarily a reflection on Grey's choice, as he would have ordered them from David Hay, it reflects at least what were considered fashionable roses at the time. Of the 11 varieties selected, only one is from an English rose tradition: a recently developed Moss rose from France called Princess Adelaide, bred in 1845. The rest are a mix of Chinas (Louis Phillipe), Bourbons, Teas, and Hybrid Perpetuals, with only one recognisable today — the classic Tea rose, Devoniensis, a pretty blush-pink rose bred in England, in Devon naturally, by Foster in 1838.

The grand presence of roses that made them a must for Government House also endeared them to the speculators who were drawn to New Zealand to make a quick profit on capital in the high risk, high profit colonial economy. Roses provided image, growing and flowering rapidly to enhance the property they graced with a civilising touch of suitable colour, or to soften the hard edges of a new building with a graceful scramble of foliage and flowers.

A perfect rose to embellish a new house at the time was the exotic Asian rose, *Rosa banksiae*. Named after Mrs Banks when it was first taken to England from China in 1807, and available in single and double white forms as well as yellow, this rose has wonderful advantages for someone wanting a quick result: it is a rapid grower, with evergreen, dark, glossy foliage, it is thornless, and the double white flowers that flash in early spring bring with them a heavenly fragrance.

Lady Barker, who arrived with her second husband in Christchurch in 1865, was a keen observer of the Canterbury district in which she spent three years. In her book, *Station Life in New Zealand*,

Mesopotamia is a high country station famous as the home of writer Samuel Butler, who in the manner of early sheep station speculators developed the property to sell it, four years later, for a considerable profit. The limited garden at Mesopotamia shortly after the sale is typical of the minimum effort made on high country homesteads at the time.
Mesopotamia c. 1871 (Alexander Turnbull Library)

written in the form of letters and published after she left New Zealand, she captures some of the essence of Canterbury country gardens at the time, and their efforts to create a suitably genteel atmosphere at odds with the countryside. Roses play an important part in this, and *R. banksiae* features in her first garden description, adding a touch of romance to the terribly English situation.

I found myself saying constantly, in a sort of ecstasy, 'How I wish they could see this in England!' and not only see it, but feel it, for the very breath one draws on such a morning is a happiness; the air is so light and yet balmy, it seems to heal the lungs as you inhale it. The verandah is covered with honeysuckles and other creepers, and the gable end of the house where the bow-window of the drawing-room projects, is one mass of yellow Banksia roses in full blossom. A stream runs through the grounds, fringed with weeping willows, which are in their greatest beauty at this time of the year, with their soft, feathery foliage of the tenderest green. The flower beds are dotted about the lawn, which surrounds the house and slopes away from it...Then, in the front, the country stretches away in undulating downs to a chain of high hills in the distance: every now and then there is a deep gap in these, through which you see magnificent snow-covered mountains.

Heathstock Station was her grandest visit, but there were other gardens and roses that enlivened her sense of English rural calm amidst a strange landscape, and her own desire to have her garden prepared in a similar way. 'There is a large, wide veranda round two sides of the house, with French windows opening into it; and I could not help feeling impatient to see my own creepers in such luxuriant beauty as these roses and honeysuckles were.'

Roses in particular seemed to epitomise the life of an ordered garden, 'the very roses, growing like a red fringe on the skirts of the great Bush, seemed awaking to fresh life and perfume.'

In spite of Lady Barker's enthusiasm for roses during her brief time in Canterbury, and the rapid expansion of the nursery business in Christchurch during the 1850s and 1860s, no substantial private rose garden was created. The transience of many early station owners meant gardens were developed as short-term investments, rather than the far-sighted creations of European landowners who expected their descendants to retain a family hold on their land. Roses were planted arbitrarily, and while some very old roses, especially resilient climbers, are still to be found on a few of the large properties, there was no tradition of New Zealand rose gardening created by large property owners at this time. It was left to later owners of these grand estates to develop the elaborate rose gardens that their size and wealth assumed.

The great public gardens were similarly mean in contributing to a rose tradition. Between 1890 and 1897, large areas of land were set aside for public gardens and domains in Dunedin, Oamaru, Christchurch, Nelson, Wellington, Palmerston North, New Plymouth and Auckland, with much energy and money being spent on them. The history of each provides an interesting view of colonial New Zealand's art and ambitions, and the wide range of experimentation and collection that was needed to develop these gardens, but they were none of them serious rose gardens. Until a formal rose garden was developed in Hagley Park, Christchurch, in 1910, the public domains played no part in establishing a colonial rose gardening tradition. They expended their energies instead on botanic collection and an expansive form of design that had its origins in the manipulated landscapes of Capability Brown's England. The city politicians, it seems, were concerned with high science and high art in their gardening ventures.

It was left to the large number of modest private gardeners to work on roses, along with a few illustrious city estates like those of Wilson and Brett in Auckland. To these gardeners, the nurserymen supplied the most modern roses available, and roses became a popular passion in New Zealand before they were an elite one; a popularity which has caused the great New Zealand gardens to follow, rather than lead, and which has been the outstanding feature of rose growing in New Zealand.

In Christchurch, where nurseries sprang up as quickly as the plants they sold, there were eight major nursery businesses and roses were a feature of almost all of them. The first of them, William Wilson, offered roses in his first advertisement placed in the *Lyttleton Times* in September 1851, as well as Sweet Briars for hedging at 10/- per dozen. By 1876 Wilson claimed to have 300 rose varieties available; by 1877 his largest competitor in the rose business, Thomas Abbott, who had opened his gates in 1859 and who was considered an expert rosarian, had 25,000 rose trees in his nursery.

Abbott's advertising was still claiming the same number of trees in 1886, by which time his was the pre-eminent rose growing operation in the South Island, supplying gardeners throughout Canterbury as well as selling roses to other nurseries around the country. He offered the latest roses from France and England: the first of the Hybrid Teas, including the famous La France, thought to be the first of the new family which was bred by Jean-Baptiste Guillot in Lyon in 1865; Noisettes; Bourbons; Chinas; Portlands; and an enormous range of Hybrid Perpetuals, which had by this time come to dominate the rose world.

The Hybrid Perpetuals are the real 'old roses' of New Zealand. The first roses, the Chinas and Sweet Briar, were not here particularly because they were roses, but because their functions served the time. Those that followed during the establishment period were the pioneers of garden roses in New Zealand, but were really traditional English roses that simply bridged a gap, as they were already slipping from their dominance in England by the time New Zealand was declared a colony. Some which arrived here during that time might have a more interesting claim to a strong New Zealand connection, especially Sanguinea, if any proof of its precise history could be found, but these are exceptions to the flow of our rose history rather than part of it.

Hybrid Perpetuals and their modern French supporters, the Noisettes and the Bourbons, made New Zealand a rose place because of the support they aroused amongst ordinary gardeners, from Dunedin to the Bay of Islands. They were, however, a quickly passing fancy, for they began a trend towards capriciousness that has become a characteristic of the rose world. From their vast number very few have survived as classics, and only Ard's Rover, Gloire de Ducher, Mme Victor Verdier, Victor Verdier, Triomphe de l'Exposition, and the archetypal Hybrid Perpetual, Reine des Violettes, can now be readily found in this country. These, and the glorious white rose, Frau Karl Druschki, which was produced at the end of the Hybrid Perpetual age in 1901, can still be found in a few specialist rose nurseries that have kept traces of our colonial rose heritage alive.

Many of the great Hybrid Perpetuals that commanded respect in their time have now disappeared completely, are hidden in private gardens, or are neglected and unknown in old corners of our cities and towns. Souvenir du Docteur Jamain, Star of Waltham, Sidonie, La Reine, Duke of Wellington, Baronnesse Rothschild, Senateur Vaisse, and General Jacqueminot were once highly rated here, as famous in their time as Peace, Iceberg and Sexy Rexy are now. They were replaced by other fashionable roses, which have in turn been replaced, and the history of New Zealand's roses, which should be alive in our gardens, has almost disappeared with those once-famous names.

General Jacqueminot's popularity spans the colonial years of New Zealand roses. The classic red rose of its time, it was bred in 1853 by the French hybridiser, Roussel, and appeared as early as 1860 on William Hale's list. Shortly afterwards, an early Montpellier Nursery catalogue included it; it appeared again in 1865, when it was described as 'most brilliant crimson, scarlet, even surpassing Geant des Batailles, the best in this class', and a catalogue from Sydney of 1866 listed it as 'rich brilliant crimson scarlet, very fine.'

As late as 1882, when Sir George Grey's gardener, Mr Osborne, was purchasing roses for the garden at Mansion House, he bought General Jacqueminot, as well as the classic Hybrid Tea, La France, showing that the General's popularity continued 30 years after its first release, when many of its compatriots had faded. It was not until the Hybrid Teas had

Roses were an important part of fashion around the turn of the century, for both men and women. Picture hats in particular were a perfect stage for roses, and for men, the buttonhole added a touch of colour, even romance, to dour suits.
(Alexander Turnbull Library)

completely taken over from the Hybrid Perpetuals that General Jacqueminot was replaced by a new generation of red roses.

This generation was the creation of a talented group of European rose breeders who refined their art with the same flair that had characterised the rose masters of Empress Josephine. The newcomers had the benefit of over half a century of rose experimentation and propagation as a foundation for their ongoing experiments, and they refined their breeding procedures by paying greater attention to the detail of their work and by using more of the horticultural knowledge accumulated by science. The result of these efforts was a group of new roses even more spectacular than their predecessors, more practical, varied, colourful, versatile and glamorous than even Josephine could have imagined.

As with the Noisettes, Bourbons and Hybrid Perpetuals of their predecessors, Europe's avant-garde rosarians had agents who quickly introduced their creations to New Zealand gardens, and they flourished in a country where the universality of rose growing had become a garden tradition by the beginning of the twentieth century. The private gardener and the flower-growing public were the forces shaping the development of roses by this time, influences which had shaped New Zealand's rose industry from the beginning, and which governed the assessment of incoming roses by the colony's specialist rose nurseries. As the hobby gardener's needs gained more value in the minds of Europe's rose breeders, so the roses they created became more suitable for the particular demands of New Zealand's rose community.

In the private gardens that were already a feature of New Zealand, roses were universally valued as worthy and often prestigious garden plants. Like the country itself, these gardens were a mix of new imagination, practical compromise and transposed establishment, and roses seemed to fit every colonial garden situation. Climbers and ramblers grew lustily and softened new buildings without imposing any rigorous gardening regime on their occupiers, and can often be seen in photographs of the time tumbling across the edges of country cottages and grand mansions with equal vigour. Most gardens were more of a personal indulgence than a planned exercise, incorporating climbers and rose trees as they fitted in amongst the other collected plants, their appeal entirely random.

Designed gardens were not common, but each town had at least a few show gardens, planned to the accepted fashions according to particular species and varieties of plants, as well as form. Worked by a professional gardener, or simply by an attentive property owner, they presented to the passing public a proper display of neatly clipped lawns and hedges, colourful borders and the elegance of roses, either restrained standards or more flamboyant bushes.

Whatever the situation, roses were used singly and were rarely, if ever, massed to use their colour to maximum effect. The choice of roses was always a personal one, made according to the influences of fashion, colour preferences, the simple likes and dislikes of the gardener, and most critically, the actual performance of each plant. As roses were so universal, and individuals invariably worked their own gardens, the susceptibility of each variety to disease and local conditions, and the consistency, shape and fragrance of their flowers, were important factors in their success.

Horticultural precision was valued, and flower shows similar to those in Europe, in which display blooms were prepared to meet the judges in the best of conditions, were common in all the main centres. The first Auckland Horticultural Society flower show, held in 1862, featured seven categories of roses, including red or purple, white, and yellow classes, and altogether occupied a quarter of the entire event. In future years the November show of the Society was held primarily for roses, which were expected to be a special feature for the public; the March event had a special section for Noisettes.

Shows certainly helped to sell roses initially, and prizes were helpful to new varieties, but it was ultimately the performance in the garden that ensured a rose had a long and profitable time on the market — that,

Roses planted on graves reflect the ancient association between roses and death, and in well-established cemeteries like this in Wellington, it is a tradition that has preserved some of the oldest roses. Bolton Street Cemetery, adjacent to Wellington Botanic Gardens, is now recognised as an 'old' rose repository of considerable importance that attracts many visitors during the summer flowering period. (Alexander Turnbull Library)

and the rose's ability to serve needs beyond the competition hall. One rose that appeared at the beginning of the new age of rose growing in 1881 illustrated just how successful a rose could be if it appealed to a popular audience, particularly in New Zealand.

Mme Cecile Brunner was released by Joseph Pernet-Ducher just after he changed his name from Pernet on his marriage to the boss's daughter, Marie Ducher, and has romantically assumed the name The Sweetheart Rose (although not necessarily in reference to that occasion). Its tiny flowers have never won any famous awards, but it has charmed four generations of rose growers around the world with its delightfully prim little buds and blooms of sweet pink. It is the perfect rose for a buttonhole, a fashion that enhanced its popularity in New Zealand where every well-dressed gent's lapel carried a flower. It continues to sell and to be favoured in gardens 90 years after it was first sent to the bottom of the world.

Joseph Pernet-Ducher was the first of the new breeders, a group that discarded the rather arbitrary hybridising procedures that remained little changed from those of the Renaissance Dutch gardeners who had happened on Centifolias over 300 years previously. The vast jungle of Hybrid Perpetuals had sprung from this method, but, inspired by the techniques of an English cattleman, Henry Bennett, Pernet-Ducher and his compatriots planned the parentage of their creations more precisely by meticulous hand-fertilisation and selection from the offspring. In this way, they were able to decide precisely the characteristics they required in a rose and select parents to help them achieve that goal. For the first time since roses were bred specifically for gardens, the outcome was a matter of inspiration and planning rather than luck.

Appropriately, the arrival of New Zealand's own rose aristocrat coincided with the release of Cecile Brunner in this country, when W. E. Lippiatt began his own nursery in Walmsley Road, Otahuhu. Lippiatt was the son of one of the first rose specialists in New Zealand, Edward Lippiatt, who emigrated in 1865 from his London home to be John Logan Campbell's foreman gardener in Auckland. Shortly after he

This orderly row of standard roses gives a touch of formal pretension to the
suburban garden of this early villa.
(Alexander Turnbull Library)

arrived with his wife and three eldest sons, he began selling plants from
his two-and-a-half acre nursery in Mt Albert on his own behalf, featur-
ing raspberry plants and the latest roses. It was the beginning of an
important contribution to New Zealand rose growing.

By the mid 1870s, Edward Lippiatt was established as the leading
rose grower in Auckland and was challenging the Christchurch nursery
establishment with the range of roses he had on offer. He had already
made contact with the English firm of William Paul, a leading breeder
of the period, and his list included no less than 85 Hybrid Perpetuals, as
well as 13 Bourbons, five Noisettes and eight Teas. It was a remarkably
modern list for the time: like David Hay's lists, it contained no traditional English roses such as Mosses, Damasks or Gallicas, nor did it
have any Chinas, Banksias or Briars. Edward Lippiatt, it seems, was the
most modern of rosarians.

For a time, Edward Lippiatt was involved in the garden at the
Auckland Domain, a public park that had not given much, if any, space
to roses. During his time at the Acclimatisation Society's gardens there,
he improved the rose selection, and for some time had a nursery nearby, on land now occupied by Carlaw Park, from where he no doubt
supplied Auckland's elite rose gardeners with the most modern innova-

tions from Europe. By the time his son, William, had opened his own nursery, the Lippiatt name was well known in rose circles.

W. E. Lippiatt inherited and expanded this reputation to become the pre-eminent rose specialist in New Zealand. By 1900 he was sending roses around the country, even to Christchurch, where strong rose nurseries already flourished. In the single month of June in 1900 he sent over 1500 roses to the Christchurch nurseries of Robert Nairn and Nimmo and Blair. But it was not just as a supplier of roses that William Lippiatt is such a significant figure in New Zealand's rose history: he was also the first rose breeder of note.

In 1883, when he opened his own nursery in Otahuhu, William Lippiatt had already spent years working for his father at the Carlaw Park nursery and in Otahuhu. During this time he must have made some rose hybridising experiments, so that when he did start business on his own behalf he was able to release his own rose: Sir Robert Stout, named in honour of the Liberal politician. A bright red Hybrid Perpetual, it won the Champion Rose title at the Auckland Horticultural Show five times, and was the beginning of an impressive collection of Lippiatt roses that emerged over the next 30 years. Sir Robert Stout was joined by another bright red Hybrid Perpetual named for a Liberal leader, Dick Seddon, in 1907, a choice of colour which reflected either Lippiatt's own enthusiasm for the Liberal cause or his opinion of their shade of politics.

Other successful Lippiatt creations were the red Hybrid Perpetual, Mrs Lippiatt, and two very fine Hybrid Teas, Otahuhu Hybrid and Enterprise. Sadly these, and the other ten Lippiatt roses, have all disappeared, unless they survive in some old garden whose treasure has not yet been identified. William Lippiatt, however, set an example as a new type of pioneer for the colony, a person whose creativity and affinity with roses matched that of his contemporaries in Europe, evidenced by his release of a Polyantha rose, Bessie Warner, in 1890, at that time a category at the leading edge of rose breeding. His achievement was recognised in 1907 by Northern Ireland's famous Dickson nursery, when

Iceberg
Vivian Ward

they named a rose W. E. Lippiatt in his honour.

W. E. Lippiatt could not have created a nursery specialising in roses if there had not been a market for the roses he offered, or the ones he bred. The nationwide success of that nursery confirms the popularity of roses in the country at that time, and the adventurous nature of gardeners to whom Lippiatt sold the latest and most advanced varieties, including his own. Lippiatt showed that New Zealand could have its own indigenous rose community, and took the new country into the twentieth century with the prospect of becoming a centre of rose activity. The climate and soils were right, the example was set; all that was required was for somebody to follow William Lippiatt's example.

W. E. Lippiatt was New Zealand's first rose breeder of note, and through his widespread rose trading he became a key figure in establishing the popularity of garden roses in this country.

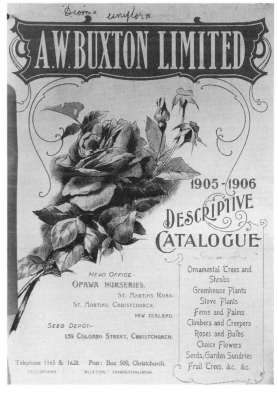

As well as contributing substantially to garden design, Buxton's garden business was one of the largest rose suppliers in the South Island, and like other nursery businesses of the time, catalogues were distributed widely and plants supplied by mail order.
(Alexander Turnbull Library)

7 Popular passion

Skyrocket burst of hardened steel
A charming light on this fair place
These technicians tricks appeal
Mixing with courage a little grace

Two star shells first
In rose pink burst
Two breasts you lay bare with a laugh
Offer their insolent tips

    HERE LIES
ONE WHO COULD LOVE
    some epitaph

A poet in the forest sees
Indifferent able to cope
His revolver catch at safe
Roses dying of their hope

Thinks of Saadi's roses then
Bows his head draws down his lip
As a rose reminds him of
The softer curving of a hip

The air is full of a terrible
Liquor from half shut stars distilled
Projectiles stroke the soft nocturnal

Perfume with your image filled
Where the roses are all killed

Gala – To André Rouveyre, *Guillaume Apollinaire (trans. Oliver Bernard)*

New Zealand arrived at the twentieth century feeling very British, and the notion that England's rose emblem had patriotic value helped promote rose growing. For at least half this century, Britain was New Zealand's anchor to Western Europe and to the civilisation New Zealanders considered they were part of, complete with its artistic and social entourage, and its roses. In spite of the turmoil the twentieth century has brought, the persistence of that attitude has secured a cultural base for roses here; the ability of garden roses to continue to adapt to social change has ensured their ever-increasing popularity.

There are many reasons why roses had become so popular by 1900. It was partly due to the ease with which roses can be grown in almost every part of the country, partly because of the high status roses had in the most pretentious of colonial gardens, and partly because roses, dripping as they are with sentimentality, were such a powerful icon of domestic art at the time. Taking these factors into account, it seems hardly necessary to consider how much breeders were a factor, making roses to suit changing values. But by 1900 roses were no longer simply beautiful, they were fashionably beautiful.

Roses were perfectly situated to take advantage of the next stage of the colonisation of New Zealand: the taking of the country-side. Although New Zealand now had many cities and towns, complete with the benefits and disadvantages of urban life, ordered New Zealand still clung to the coasts, with a large and wild beast of bush and gullies lurking in the country's centre. Between 1890 and 1930 that beast was tamed as 5 million hectares of countryside were broken in. Bush was burned, cleared and planted in grass. The planner of landscapes, Capability Brown, would have been astonished by the scale of transformation from bush to farm, and by the bones of dead trees that littered the countryside for decades afterwards.

Farm makers were also garden makers, for wherever the trees came down and grass seed went in, houses were built, and around houses, gardens. As in the towns these gardens were part of the home, cut off from the surrounding countryside, from the business of farming, by a fence, within which fruit trees, vegetables and 'Mum's glory', the flower garden, thrived. A drive through any stretch of rural New Zealand today reveals a procession of trimmed and nurtured gardens amongst paddocks of green, oases of domestic calm amidst the green grind of toil and mortgage. These gardens are the folk art of the generation of New Zealanders who made this country's agricultural landscape, and, only slightly modified, of the generations that succeeded them.

As in the countryside, so also in the towns as the urban population exploded. From 1896 the proportion of the population living in towns larger than 8000 people grew from slightly less than 30 per cent of the total to 49 per cent in 1936. At the same time the total population more than doubled, so that in 1936 there were more urban dwellers in New Zealand than there were in the entire country in 1896. Those 40 years represent the greatest period of change in New Zealand history, a change which saw the creation of a particularly agricultural landscape, based primarily on small farms, and of modern towns and cities in which a feature was the 'garden' suburb.

As well as these physical changes there was also a profound change to the social character of New Zealand, as the family became predominant for the first time. In towns and cities, the family was the focus for married couples, about which a secure home where children could be nurtured assumed almost exclusive priority. Similarly in the country, especially on newly formed small farms where dairying and raising fat lambs for export involved total family involvement, the home was the family base. These were perfect conditions for the development of a strong gardening culture, infused as people already were by the colonial tradition of affinity with the land, and the far older one of the garden as a refuge.

The popularity of roses during this period was unprecedented, and there was more development than at any previous time in New Zealand's rose history. Already roses were in a strong position as a garden flower, and the increase in private gardening activity simply strengthened that position. There were a number of other events during the first part of this century, however, which accentuated the status of roses and ensured their continued success in spite of the dramatic influences of depression and war, or perhaps because of them.

Early on, the Western European civilisation to which New Zealand clung so tenaciously in 1900 had its passions exposed by bloody war between 1914 and 1918. While this event no doubt contributed to an assumption that the country had through conflict acquired a callow nationhood, it also served to reinforce the patriotic dimension of the English rose as a powerful symbol of Empire. Simultaneously, war served up the most painful aspects of the rose mystery — transience and death — and enhanced the maudlin aspects of sentimental rose mythology. War was as good for roses as it was for poets.

Patriotism has, like so many other ideologies based on faith, made good use of the rose in many countries; what was the most English emblem at the heart of Empire epitomised Gallic grace and style to the

Careful formality, almost in imitation of Tudor gardens in the strictness of line and severe trim, was typical of rose gardening before the Second World War. Christchurch's pristine civic gardens were one of the first and amongst the most widely respected of all New Zealand's public rosaries.

French. The fanfare of that British Empire was never more clearly sounded than in the original objectives of the National Rose Society, which was formed in 1931, to 'implant roses in the hearts and gardens of the people...[and] to induce gardeners to specialise in roses, the floral emblem of England.'

The formation of the National Rose Society was the culmination of a period of public exaltation of roses, which for a time replaced the botanic collection and landscape themes of public parks around the country. In Christchurch, a public rose garden was made in 1910, the first such public garden in the country and a celebration of the highest form of rose garden design. This had various selected rose varieties planted in beds, one variety per bed to maximise the impact of the flowers. The beds were formally laid out in precise lines or neatly spoked circles around a central circular bed, each bordered with clipped, low box hedges, and set in a space of pristine lawn.

The Christchurch Rose Garden, under the direction of the Christchurch Botanic Garden curator, James Young, was a fine example of the ornately formal style that was presumed appropriate for a plant as important as the rose. Prim standards were a feature of the planting, in preference to more unruly bushes, and the natural tumbling character of roses was restricted to displays of climbers, ramblers or pillar roses on arches, fences and other specially constructed supports. It was a period in which roses gained a formality that the rest of the garden was escaping from, and it was repeated in the public rose gardens built in all the main cities and towns within 20 years of the opening of the Christchurch Rose Garden.

Although Wellington and Auckland had well established public gardens by 1900, neither had paid much attention to roses (other than the selection of roses that flourished in the Acclimatisation Society garden in the Auckland Domain during Edward Lippiatt's tenure as curator). The Auckland Domain has never featured a rose garden, but Wellington's Botanic Gardens began development of an exclusive rose area in 1901; by 1917, the Rosary was complete. Again the beds,

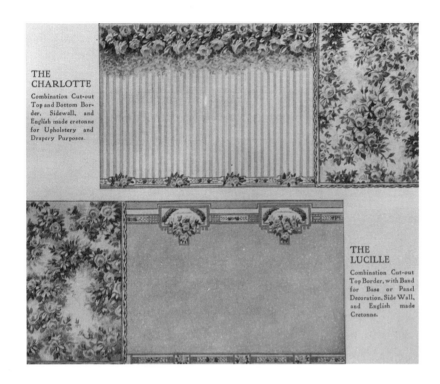

'The Charlotte' and 'The Lucille' were two lavish rose-patterned wallpapers being offered to homeowners in 1915, indicating that the flower of Venus was already well established as a feature of domestic design. Furnishings, bedding, china and even cutlery still carry rose devices, a timeless symbol of prettiness that has been usurped by merchandisers everywhere. (Alexander Turnbull Library)

frequently planted with standards, were edged with box and an air of formality dominated but, unlike Christchurch, various bedding plants softened and reduced the sterile appearance conveyed by standards in tenaciously cultivated blocks.

Ultimately, the Rosary was replaced by a much larger and only slightly less formal design when the now-famous Lady Norwood Rose Garden was completed in 1953 after three years of careful work. This has survived to remain one of the finest rose gardens in the country, and for 40 years has provided an ongoing display of modern roses growing in Wellington conditions. Like the Christchurch Rose Garden, the Lady Norwood retains elements of the careful formality of rose garden design from the first half of this century.

Dunedin has never had a formal public rose garden, in spite of the example set by neighbouring Oamaru when the council gave permission for a rose garden to be laid out in 1924. Queen's Gardens in Nelson also introduced a full rose garden in the 1920s, completing work in 1923, and Auckland finally made a show of roses in 1934 after the Auckland City Council donated land at Parnell for a rose garden. Auckland nurseries gave 3000 plants, from which a garden was created in the formal pattern, with massed beds of roses bordered by pohutukawa. Now famous as the Parnell Rose Garden, it is, in November and December when the trees are crimson with pre-Christmas blossom, a spectacular display of roses in a New Zealand setting.

While public rose gardens were presenting the rose to urban New Zealanders as a valued plant, rose gardens themselves had assumed the high cultural value that had been allotted to botanic collections last century. In effect, an increasingly democratic country was formalising the popular art of flower gardening by institutionalising its most elite form. Indeed, while roses were certainly popular, they were also a statement of elitism; the formal rose garden on private property became as much a status symbol as the automobile, especially along urban streets where the ethos of each home was presented by the garden to passing traffic.

In the most grandiose of gardens roses were a separate feature, a corner of indulgence that reflected the secret rose garden of medieval times. The leading landscape designer and nurseryman of the time, Alfred Buxton of Christchurch, played an important role in popularising this style of rosary amongst the landed gentry with whom he had considerable influence. He was responsible for designing gardens throughout the country, and left a lasting impression in Canterbury, Hawke's Bay, Poverty Bay and the Wairarapa, where he was often engaged by wealthy farmers to give their properties a sense of grace. His gardens are amongst the most elegant in the country, especially now they can be seen in a state of maturity, and they give to New Zealand gardening an element of proportion that was generally lacking in the gardens of the great colonial estates.

Buxton's designs also perpetuated the special nature of roses, for he invariably included roses in a secret garden format that enhanced their particular importance. Carefully formal without being severe, these rosaries were usually separated from the rest of the garden by a subtle device that did not interfere with the complete garden's lines, often by making them sunken gardens. The sense of seclusion was further enhanced by working them into a corner next to the house, so that they gave the impression of being intimate extensions of the private living area.

Buxton made rose gardens that reflected the social status of roses at the time, and also captured some of the character of their European and New Zealand history. The extreme version of rose elitism, however, was as blatant and ugly as Buxton's was reserved and stylish: a clumsy formal style that cluttered so many gardens in vain imitation of Buxton and the public rosaries, imposed on the constrained suburban quarte-acre. Neatly arranged beds set in clipped lawns looked claustrophobic when forced between the close hedges or fences of subdivision, and many polite suburban houses appeared ridiculous behind such pretentious fuss. Much of the dislike of roses that exists today is a consequence of this awkward treatment, which can still be seen in the sad line of tawdry standards that too often haunts the edges of garden paths and drives.

The expanding population of the early twentieth century brought new homes and gardens, which needed nurseries to supply their plants and other gardening needs. The nurserymen who had built up their businesses in the last years of the previous century thrived amidst the prosperity of expansion. For specialist plants such as roses, mail order became an important part of business, for there were few nurseries in the thriving small towns and the country customer was now very big business indeed.

Urban expansion was also taking a new form, one with encouraging prospects for nurseries: the development of 'garden' suburbs. These examples of the benefits of town planning were being made possible by the network of electric tram services found in all the major cities by 1910. Gardening was encouraged in the new suburbs, and naturally roses featured.

W. E. Lippiatt had become established as the leading rose grower in the Dominion, and his Otahuhu nurseries were busy supplying roses to private customers around the country as well as to other nurseries in the major centres. In 1908, at the summer show of the Auckland

The oasis garden, New Zealand style: a neat rural garden around a prim Californian bungalow with roses arching over the veranda stands before the bones of the forest that once occupied these hills.
(Alexander Turnbull Library)

Horticultural Society held in Old Government House, Lippiatt's roses were dominant. As well as taking the prize for Champion Rose with the Hybrid Tea, Mrs W. J. Grant, he also won six first prizes from only seven available categories, and received a very favourable review of his own new rose, May Alexandra Lippiatt, from the Weekly Gazette and N.Z. Mail of the day.

Lippiatt was the master of his trade, and even his toughest competitors carried his roses. D. A. Hay at Montpellier listed Otahuhu Hybrid, a 20-year-old Hybrid Tea described as 'extra fine', as well as May Alexandra Lippiatt and Sir Robert Stout, the two most resilient New Zealand-bred roses of the time. For another 20 years Lippiatt flourished, supplying cut roses to market as well as rose plants to his nursery customers, taking an active part in the newly formed N.Z. Association of Nurserymen, which had its first meeting in 1904, and importing, propagating and distributing the latest and best roses from Europe's leading breeders. These included Alex Dickson and Sam McGredy from Northern Ireland; Cant and Son, and William Paul from England; France's Pernet-Ducher; and H. A. Verschuren from the Netherlands.

At its peak, the Lippiatt nursery in Walmsley Road, Otahuhu, was producing over 60,000 rose plants annually for the New Zealand market, a sign of not only the success of W. E. Lippiatt but of the popularity of roses at the time. As well as Montpellier, there were a number of other competitors who before the First World War began specialising in roses to meet the demands of a rapidly expanding market, and in response to the overall size of the nursery market that was now able to support specialists. In 1911 the Cutler brothers established a nursery in New Lynn, one of the new fast-growing suburbs of Auckland; in 1912, Frank Mason set up business near Feilding. Both would play influential roles in the development of rose growing in New Zealand.

Immediately after the First World War, Whitcombe and Tombs published *Flower Gardening in New Zealand* to cater to the flourishing garden market. It was jointly written by the Christchurch Botanic Gardens curator, James Young, and D. A. Hay, who had taken over Montpellier Nurseries from his father. The book reflected the popularity of roses at the time by giving them the largest chapter of any single garden variety, more than twice the size of the dahlia or chrysanthemum sections. The authors commented, 'Roses are becoming greater favourites yearly with the introduction of so many varieties.'

These were completely different roses from those of the 1880s, however, as the book's list of recommended roses reveals. Of the 65 named, Hybrid Perpetuals account for only four, and Teas nine, while there are 13 Climbers, and 39 of the wonderfully fashionable new Hybrid Teas. Hybrid Teas may have taken some time to get going since the release of La France in 1867, but their gracefully pointed buds and high-centred, elegant blooms had completely taken over from Hybrid Perpetuals, which, with the exception of Frau Karl Druschki and a few others, had slipped into seclusion by the end of the 1920s.

Throughout the first half of this century, the rose world was absorbed in a quest for the perfect red Hybrid Tea, a rose that would epitomise roses' passion with its pure dark-red petals, and capture New Age chic with its beautifully poised buds and graceful blooms. There were many attempts by the greatest rose breeders of the day, but few real successes as new roses revealed a blue cast in their colour that faded to magenta or purple, tended to crimson, or lacked the red intensity or pristine form of a classic.

W. E. Lippiatt himself created some of the most successful pure reds, with May Alexander Lippiatt probably the best of them, and all were being sold until well into the 1930s. In the case of the Hybrid Perpetual, Mrs Lippiatt, this was 50 years after it was released, unusual longevity for a rose of that vintage. It was the Hybrid Teas that had the edge of popularity though, and of these one survived the vagaries of rose fashion throughout the 1920s and 1930s to still be considered an important rose in 1955, when the full impact of a new generation of rose breeders was having its effect in New Zealand.

Etoile de Holland was bred by the Dutch cultivist Verschuren in 1919, and released in New Zealand the following year, probably by W. E. Lippiatt, who was dealing directly with H. E. Verschuren and Sons at that time. Fragrant, with healthy foliage and gorgeously shaped buds, it was never a spectacular success but maintained a place in almost every New Zealand catalogue for the next 30 years, and was used by many nurseries for the cut flowers they supplied as a profitable sideline.

The years following the First World War were innovative times in New Zealand, and roses reflected this air of creative daring, not so much

An official painting from the First World War, which attempts to 'feminise' an otherwise sturdy, masculine composition with the rather incongruous inclusion of a vase of roses.
"Red Cross Workers, 1919", George Edward Butler (National Archives of New Zealand)

in the substance of their breeding, but in the range of colours and the variety of colour combinations that became available. This daring was evident in roses like the sensational yellow and scarlet Lady Margaret Stewart, the glowing orange and apricot Angèle Pernet, and Margaret Dickson Hamill, a pale sandy-yellow rose tinged with carmine that almost predicted the coming sensation of Peace. These were never bedding roses in the formal manner encouraged by gardening experts but exotics that encouraged collecting, and as more fantastic roses appeared so the pressure to collect increased.

Like all fashion industries, the imperative to have and flaunt the latest creation was encouraged by breeders and nurseries alike, and the whole garden pattern was made subservient to the accumulation of individual roses, a trend that has continued in New Zealand gardens, most especially rose gardens. With the collecting trend, knowledge became as important as the roses themselves: knowledge of the breeders involved, lineage of the rose, its type and preferences — the whole paraphernalia of information that creates amateur experts.

Innovation did not overwhelm the New Zealand rose world, however, but was merely an aspect of the period that reflected a particular trend, as gardens are inclined to do. New Zealand was still as entranced by pink roses as ever, a preference that continued into the 1930s. Pink roses did, however, lose a little ground to the new 'art' coloured roses with their palette-like blends, and the spectacular colour contrasts being achieved by breeders of the stature of McGredy and Dickson.

As an example of the changes in colour fashion and popularity, it is interesting to compare the rose catalogues of the early 1900s — a time when Hybrid Perpetuals were losing their predominance — and the late 1920s, by which time Hybrid Teas had gained the ascendency. Pink was certainly to the fore early on, and pink roses accounted for a massive 35 per cent of catalogue listings between 1898 and 1906. A short 20 years later, this proportion had slipped to just 25 per cent. Still significant, but a considerable fall in favour. Other discernible changes during this period were a slight increase in the number of red roses being offered,

By 1922, Wellington Botanic Garden had one of the finest formal rose gardens in the country – a prissy corner of a great, rambling expanse of botanic indulgence. (Alexander Turnbull Library)

from 20 per cent to 25 per cent of listings, and a sudden surge in the availability of yellow roses, which climbed from 18 per cent to 25 per cent.

Raw statistics are just facts, and the colour changes of the time are both more subtle and more profound than the figures show. Pink roses maintained their special place in the favours of New Zealanders, but the presence of yellow in the Hybrid Tea bloodlines was bringing forward a number of very fine yellow and pink combinations, adding a new colour category that could be principally pink or yellow depending on the state of the flower. This flow of yellow was coming directly from that old source of inspiration, France, and the breeding beds of Joseph Pernet-Ducher, whose contribution to modern roses is best described as a touch of gold.

Pernet-Ducher was not alone in his attempt to breed better yellow strains into his roses — others had been trying for almost as long as cul-

Rose lovers began to organise themselves in the twenties. Here roses are being prepared for the first Rose Day in Wellington in 1924.
(Alexander Turnbull Library)

tivists had turned their attention to roses — but his persistence was unique. After years of painstaking work with the almost infertile *Rosa foetida persiana*, he produced Soleil d'Or in 1900, giving to the brand-new twentieth century Hybrid Teas with yellow, as well as rampant oranges and fiery scarlets. These colours were already represented in abundance in the New Zealand rose nursery lists of 1930, when the flashy Mrs McGredy showed off her garish orange, yellow and red blooms for the first time, a release that lead ultimately to the greatest ever yellow/pink Hybrid Tea, for Mrs McGredy was the pollen mother of Peace.

The air of innovation that permeated the country during the 1920s, encouraging nurseries to run with the latest and most dramatic rose 'novelties', as breeders termed their newest creations, also stimulated a number of other experiments in New Zealand. These encompassed every field from new horticultural crops to economic theories,

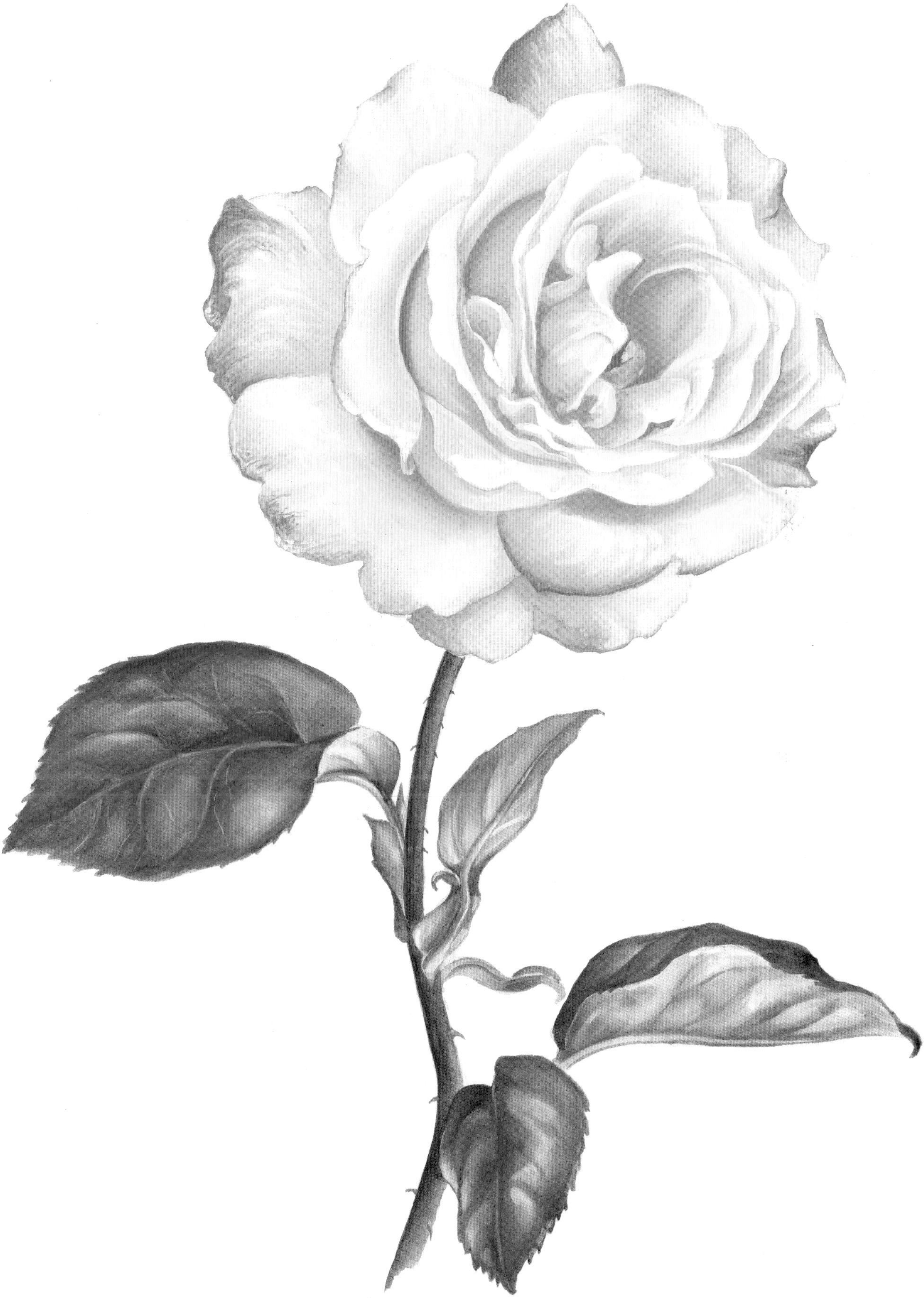

Peace
Vivian Ward

including an episode that remains one of the most bizarre in our history, and involved the Government in industrial espionage.

As the Government of the day was supportive of investigations into new crops for the huge areas of recently tamed land, in the hope that they could diversify New Zealand's economy, they attracted all sorts of ideas and schemes, including one which considered an attar of rose industry. In November 1924, the British Consul in Sofia, Bulgaria, wrote to a Mr Williams of the British Isles Association of New Zealand, who was visiting Britain at the time: 'There is another industry which does not appear to have been tried in New Zealand, and that is the culture of the Rose for the production of Attar of Roses; this is a very lucrative business, and should your friends in New Zealand be interested, I should be glad to send you cuttings of the special rose grown for this purpose, and also samples of the attar produced, as well as any information you may require on the subject.'

Incredibly, the British Consul's offer was sent to the Prime Minister, William Massey, who passed it on to the Minister of Agriculture, who in turn sought advice from his enterprising Director General, C. J. Reakes.

On 9 February 1925, the Prime Minister replied to the London enquiry: 'I should be very grateful to Mr Williams if he would accept the Consul's kind offer to supply a few plants of the special rose grown in

Prime Minister, William Massey: "I should be very grateful... if he would accept the Consul's kind offer to supply a few plants." Industrial espionage directed from the highest office of state.
(Alexander Turnbull Library)

Bulgaria for the production of Attar of Roses, and a sample of the Attar produced. An outline of the methods of harvesting the crop and making the extract would also be much appreciated.'

By this letter, the New Zealand Prime Minister, in conspiracy with the British Consul, embarked on a subterfuge to smuggle rose cuttings from Bulgaria, as well as information necessary to establish a competitive attar of rose industry in New Zealand. If neither he nor his advisors were aware of the vigour with which Bulgaria had protected its attar industry for centuries, then the British Consul certainly was. At the very least both parties must have known that cuttings or plants of the Damask rose grown for attar production in Bulgaria were banned exports.

When nothing had been heard by October 1926, the new Prime Minister, Gordon Coates (Massey had died early in 1925) sent a letter to the High Commissioner in London, prompting him to pursue the matter if it had not yet been successful. It must have been a timely reminder, for on 6 December the cuttings arrived secretly in England from Bulgaria. In poor condition, they were passed on to the Director of the Horticultural Society's gardens at Wisley in Surrey to be resurrected enough to make the long journey to New Zealand. Those involved had had no success procuring either specific information on the production of attar, or a sample for the New Zealand scientists.

Following this there was an 11-month silence from London, with neither rose plants nor attar appearing in Wellington secreted in a diplomatic pouch or a sea captain's gumboot. Again a memo from the Prime Minister to London, again a rapid response. It appears that the rose plants had indeed died in Wisley, Surrey, and in June 1926 Mr Williams was again dispatched to Bulgaria in pursuit of cuttings of *Rosa damascena* 'Kazanlik'. This time there appears to have been a mole at the consulate in Sofia, or at least the guards in the Valley of the Roses were sharper than they had been the previous year, and Mr Williams was detained at the border in the act of smuggling. Exact details of his treatment are not on record, but he duly arrived in London without the cuttings, after he had, as the New Zealand High Commission put it, 'had considerable difficulty in propitiating the authorities.'

That was effectively the end of the attar of rose experiment, dead before it started, but it could have been interesting had the investigation been less devious and more creative. It was in many ways an episode indicative of the first 25 years of this century, when so much was new and so many experiments were tried; the rose community as much as any can look back and say, 'What if...?'

8 Order

The glittering topaz in your glass
Was vintaged forty years ago;
Your emerald has seen eight kings pass,
A thousand candles glow.

Watched in a jewel, the taper curls;
The royal men, the wine that flows
Are tints and crowns; the peerless girls
Are broken shadows of a rose.

At a Danse Macabre, *Charles Spear*

There were many dreams smashed in the 1930s, those of businesses, families and individuals. It was a bleak time that wrung the confidence from people and nations, no matter how small or far away from the centre of things.

New Zealand's depression was hard, made bleaker by a widespread belief that the country was being throttled by someone else's mistakes. The bureaucracy that had grown with the country, and its politicians, was challenged by the Depression to find both economic and social solutions as politicians had been in the depression of the 1890s. When these solutions were finally put into effect, they transformed New Zealand, bringing a change in attitude as much as in social and economic organisation, and a shift from the independence of a frontier to the interdependence of twentieth-century society.

What the Depression did to gardening, and to roses, was less dramatic than the economic situation would suggest. While unemployment was widespread across the country, established farming and business enterprises were still reasonably well off and those with money were still able to indulge their fashionable whims. Contrary to popular Depression mythology, sales of some consumer goods actually increased during the 1930s, even as sales of major items of family expenditure, like cars and houses, fell drastically. While few new gardens were created, those gardens that already existed continued to be a market for rose nurseries, as roses' establishment friends looked after them well.

During the Depression years the area of land given over to nurseries changed very little; by 1936 it was much the same area as it had been in 1926. Evidence of nursery stability can be found in the minimal change in prices nurseries charged for novelty roses between 1925 and 1932, while the standard catalogue listings, which had been an area of growth in the trade, slipped slightly. Novelty roses were the favourites of the fashionable gardener with an established garden, while new gardeners bought from the general list, made up of roses already well known, or chose a starter set of rose plants assembled by nurseries for this purpose.

Between 1925 and 1932, single general catalogue listings, which had appeal for both the established gardener as replacement plants and new gardeners as 'starters', showed a 25 per cent drop in price, from 2/- to 1/6. Special selections offered by nurseries, of 12 or 24 roses suited to cutting or gardening, fell 36 per cent in price — a fair sign that the new garden market was struggling. Nevertheless, over the same period, novelties maintained their price of 5/-.

These price drops were not extreme in the context of the Depression, and indicate how steady the rose industry remained in spite of the difficult times. The collapse of W. E. Lippiatt in 1929, and his amazing reconstruction in ten years, is as good a sign as any that talented nursery operators could still make a healthy profit in spite of the economy. Sales of rose plants may not have continued to increase, as they had for over 30 years, but by the late 1930s W. E. Lippiatt was again selling 60,000 plants annually, as he had done in the mid 1920s.

The stock market crash of 1929 was followed by a worldwide

State houses accelerated the development of 'garden suburbs' during the 1930s, and introduced thousands of New Zealand families to the possibility of gardening for the first time. Initially these were practical vegetable gardens, but flowers inevitably crept in, of which roses were the ultimate indulgence.

(Alexander Turnbull Library)

slump in land prices, a slump that ruined many of New Zealand's small farmers, particularly those smallholders who had made fat lamb and dairy farming such important contributors to New Zealand's export receipts. Lippiatt's Otahuhu land suffered a spectacular drop in value just as he became involved in a land speculation deal, and he lost everything but his name as a fine nurseryman and father figure of the rose industry. That reputation was enough collateral for old W. E. Lippiatt to start again, 45 years after he had set out on his own. The bank was prepared to fund him, and with an overdraft of £10,000 he set up a new nursery in Panama Road, Pakuranga, and began to develop stocks of the plants and trees that had always been the backbone of his business: citrus, peach and apple trees, hot-house grapes, and roses. By 1936 he was again sending roses around the country, supplying small gardeners and major nurseries alike, and importing the latest 'novelties' from Dickson, McGredy, and the rest of the rose world's trendsetters.

At that time roses were despatched by post or rail to any destination in the country, with bare roots ready to plant. Each nursery had its own secret recipe for preparing the roses for travel, and at Lippiatt's each bundle of plants was dipped in a slurry of cow dung and clay mixed with water, which was then allowed to dry on the roots. This protected the roots and permitted new rootlets to form, so that the plant was ready to settle into its new environment as soon as it was planted. Once the slurry was set, the bundles were packed in sphagnum moss to help retain moisture, while offering some protection from knocks and bumps on the journey. It was not the most sophisticated packaging system, but with subtle variations it worked for almost every nursery in the country.

When old William Lippiatt died in 1941, 76 years after he had arrived in New Zealand with his parents and two brothers on the *Belgravia*, roses had completed their period of transition in this country. Through the inspiration of William Lippiatt himself the first steps had been taken towards an indigenous rose breeding industry, and a relationship between the rose and New Zealand was being shaped that was particularly its own. At the final reading of the accounts in 1941, W. E. Lippiatt had £500 in the bank, owned one of the most famous rose nurseries in the country and owed nothing. Quite a revival from the disaster of 1929, and a fair insight into the resilience of a man who can reasonably be called the father of the New Zealand rose.

Lippiatt was not the only rose specialist who struggled through the Depression years, keeping roses to the fore for the gardening booms of 1950s and 1960s. Hosking and Hollinger had made a name for their Papakura nursery by the early 1930s, enthusiastically promoting a range that was only slightly smaller than Lippiatt's. David Hay kept up the competition from Montpellier, and both Cutler's and Hayward Wright's New Lynn nurseries were active in one of Auckland's fastest growing suburban districts. In New Plymouth, Duncan and Davies had a healthy mail-order trade, and the Christchurch nurseries, while they bought many of their roses from Lippiatt, remained very successful competitors in Canterbury's strong and stable garden market.

Few of these competitors were rose specialists to the extent that Lippiatt was, however. None had made the same contacts with leading European breeders that ensured early and regular supplies of the latest 'novelties'; none provided the detailed descriptions and careful performance analysis that was so often needed with regular introductions of large numbers of new roses into previously untested conditions. None, that is, but Frank Mason.

IF I SHOULD PLANT A TINY SEED OF LOVE (No. 1).

Busy little honey bees were buzzing to and fro,
  Humming in the summer air,
Gathering the honey and the little drops of dew
  That lay within the blossoms fair,
A youth and a maid through a garden strayed,
  And the youth seemed out of sorts,
So the maid, with a smile, just to tease him said:
  "I'll give a penny for your thoughts."—
  "I was wondering," said he.

PHOTO ONLY COPYRIGHT 1909   BY ARRANGEMENT WITH B. MACDONALD, J. W. TATE & B. FELDMAN & CO.
BY BAMFORTH & CO.

The popular image of roses in this early twentieth-century postcard are
recognisably the same old story of love, sexual innuendo and the quiet luxury of a
secret garden.
"If I should plant a tiny seed of love" (Alexander Turnbull Library)

FOLLOWING PAGES: The Buxton-designed garden at Washpool in Hawke's Bay
clearly shows the medieval twist he often gave the rose garden. Lush and almost
secret in the way it was divided from the rest of the garden, it retains its intimacy
by being fitted close to the living area of the house.

The central rose in this painting may be symbolic of the artist's femininity, but it also appears to have a more personal, immediate dimension to it. Hodgkins's own fondness for Spain and southern France suggests she had more than a passing knowledge of the potency of the rose image, and its religious role, but how much of this is invested here is difficult to judge.

"Self-portrait", Frances Hodgkins (Auckland City Art Gallery)

Frank was of staunch colonial gardening stock, his father, 'Quaker' Mason, the owner of an impressive 6-hectare garden at Avalon, in the Hutt Valley, had one of the most important botanic collections in the country last century. In 1912, Frank Mason moved to Feilding, where he established himself as a nurseryman, selling a wide range of plants, fruit trees and shrubs, and early on displayed an affinity for roses. Like the Lippiatts, who were responsible for the introduction of pepinos, Frank's experimental nature saw him become the first nurseryman to grow Chinese gooseberries for fruit and so play a part in the development of the kiwi fruit industry. Again, like the Lippiatts, Frank also ran a general nursery, and while his reputation as a rose specialist became a feature of his business, it never took over completely. By the 1930s, Frank Mason was one of New Zealand's most respected rosarians. In the period immediately before and after the Second World War he was a leader in the rose community as it became better co-ordinated and, in keeping with the times, more orderly.

When the New Zealand National Rose Society was formed in Auckland in November 1931, the only unusual aspect of the event was that it had taken so long to happen. In a country where committee forming has been a national sport since at least the 1880s, and given the propensity of roses to harbour pretension, as well as the close contact between New Zealand and Britain, it is amazing that the establishment of such a body should come 55 years after the founding of the Royal National Rose Society in Britain.

The formation of the Society followed the visit of an Englishman, Mr H. Morse, who addressed a gathering of local rosarians at Auckland University's Botany Lecture Theatre in 1929. He floated the idea of a local society amongst his hosts, who no doubt had been considering the matter for some time, and after a number of discussions amongst interested parties in various towns and cities outside Auckland, and having confirmed support in the city, a decision was made to proceed. At the inaugural meeting in Auckland, Mr D. Nathan was elected first President and Mr Frank Penn, an active amateur rosarian, Secretary.

The New Zealand National Rose Society was formed as a promotional body for roses, 'to implant roses in the hearts and gardens of the people,' as the preamble to the minutes of the first meeting said. It was also a handy collection of like minds, who, once organised, were able to communicate regularly through special publications, to disseminate information about roses, and to act as a lobby group. They have also, particularly through their lobbying activities, been able to stimulate research into the suitability of roses for local conditions, and other areas of concern to rose growers.

The new Society's first success was spectacular, and came very quickly. As the original organisation was essentially Auckland-based, the lack of an Auckland rose garden was quickly drawn to the attention of the city's politicians. The new Society's members lobbied for the creation of an Auckland rose garden, and it seems their influence was enough to gain a positive response from the Auckland City Council. After a series of protracted discussions, the often difficult task of transforming political agreement in principle into realistic action was successfully achieved, and a site was provided.

It was agreed that if the council supplied the site and planted the garden, the National Rose Society would select appropriate varieties and supply the roses. Work began on what has become the Parnell Rose Gardens in 1932, less than a year after the Society was formed, displaying a level of enthusiasm for roses that was quite remarkable given the country's depressed emotions at the time. Following preparation of the beds, the first 1000 roses, all donated by various nurseries around the Auckland region, were planted in August 1932. When a further 2000 were planted the next year, they included a donation from Frank Mason in Feilding — a sign that the new Society, although based in Auckland, was already becoming a national body in influence, if not yet in the spread of its membership.

That Parnell Garden has become a feature of the New Zealand rose community, of importance to gardeners in the large Auckland area as a trial ground, as well as a cultural treasure for the wider community, who

Parnell Rose Garden in Auckland was the first tangible evidence of the newly formed Rose Society. Today it is a feature of the city, and attracts rose growers from throughout the country.

(Alexander Turnbull Library)

make considerable recreational use of the garden and its adjacent Judges Bay park area. The trial garden facility was one of the first uses Parnell's planners intended, and in 1934 the Australian Rose Annual, which went to all New Zealand National Rose Society members until their own annual was first published in 1964, carried a review of the earliest results from Parnell, written by Frank Penn.

The Parnell experience endorsed the need for trial grounds in the minds of nurserymen and gardeners. The closure of Lippiatt's nursery with the old man's death in 1941 was the end of New Zealand's first rose-breeding operation, and there was not to be another serious attempt for 30 years. In the meantime, the latest roses being introduced were bred in and for European and North American conditions, and it was some time after their arrival in New Zealand before their performance here could be ascertained. In spite of this, roses were being sold as soon after their arrival as possible to meet demand for currently fashionable names and blooms, often with disappointing consequences.

Parnell and other similar civic gardens could have served a dual function as trial grounds, but very little of their land was realistically available. Civic gardens needed to be civic show places to justify their expense, and trials for the benefit of the rose community were a secondary consideration. Similarly nursery-conducted trials were open to accusations of bias, and included only those roses which the nursery in question had an interest in releasing and marketing. It was quickly apparent that a well organised, centrally located trial ground was essential.

The discussions and lobbying for such a facility continued for a number of years; in 1944, with considerable assistance from Frank Mason, Massey Agricultural College in Palmerston North decided to substantially expand its rose garden and use it for experimental purposes. Four thousand stocks were budded that year, and in 1945 5000 cuttings were planted, bringing to 200 the number of varieties planted at the College. While this was never specifically a trial ground, and did not have an ongoing programme of new rose introductions but rather facilitated a wide range of experiments with rose culture, it was at least a step in the right direction.

The New Zealand National Rose Society did not have any direct involvement in the Massey College garden, which was perhaps one of the reasons it gradually lost its experimental function and shrank back to a decorative role less than ten years later. The Society finally achieved the trial garden dream in 1969, when the National Rose Trial Ground opened in Palmerston North with trial beds of 58 Hybrid Teas, 31 Floribundas, eight Climbers and seven Miniatures, altogether a total of 480 plants. The trial programme has each rose in the ground for two years, extended from 18 months in 1972, following which they are replaced by new varieties. The most successful after assessment under Palmerston North conditions, which the Society consider to be a good average of New Zealand soils and climates in general, are awarded gold medals, with a premium award, the 'Gold Star of the Pacific', going to outstanding performers.

The results have given New Zealanders a regular guide to the flowering habits, growth and susceptibility to disease of a wide range of new roses. What they have not provided is a way of ascertaining the popularity of any rose, for public taste remains the one factor in rose breeding that only inspiration can address. Great roses are those that are able to transcend the idiosyncrasies of fashion, to hold the public's imagination for a long period of time, irrespective of trends.

In 1946, the Dickson Hybrid Tea Shot Silk was voted the 'Community rose' in Auckland, in a poll conducted by the Society. It was at that time 22 years old, one of the family of pink and yellow roses that were so popular through the 1920s, and, to New Zealand taste, pre-

War work. A woman gardener taking care of roses at the Auckland railway station during the Second World War; it is both a sign of the times and of the future, and as the role of women changes, so does their most persistent symbol.
(Alexander Turnbull Library)

dominantly pink. It was a feature of Society public relations work at the time, but has subsequently disappeared from most gardens.

It is appropriate that the New Zealand Rose Annual's first results of a national ballot on favourite roses, in 1964, featured Shot Silk, albeit well down the list. Another rose that appeared on that first list was Iceberg, at the beginning of its remarkable career rather than at the end, a career that is phenomenal because, unlike Shot Silk, Iceberg has none of the characteristics that one would assume would make it popular in New Zealand.

Bred by the great German house of Kordes and released in 1958, Iceberg is a Floribunda, a category of rose that burst on the scene in the mid 1920s as the result of the pioneering work of outstanding Danish cultivists, Dines and Svend Poulsen. This new rose family has a unique cluster flowering habit that covers the plants in blooms, a habit which endeared them early on to gardeners and promised success for nurseries who saw great sales opportunities for a new rose with such abundance.

For a number of years the new roses were known as Poulsen roses, because they were so distinct from any other type at the time. This name shows clearly how the leading rose breeders dominated thinking, as well as commerce, in the international rose community. As competitive rose breeders began making their own releases of this new type, the name was displaced by alternatives that were less advantageous to the Poulsen company; for a while, Polyantha was popular. Floribunda, however, was more descriptive, and it gained widespread support following its introduction by the United States firm of Jackson and Perkins in the 1930s.

More than any other family, Floribundas reflected the mood of the twentieth century, which gave preference to abundance over the singular elegance epitomised by the stylish shape of the Hybrid Teas. Floribundas' easy care nature also enhanced their support amongst a new class of urban property owners who had the land, but not necessarily the expertise, to garden. This group was the first to gain universal access to the 'cottage garden' ideal that had been nurtured by generations of British communities since the industrial revolution, and as the suburbs that fostered cottage gardening spread around New Zealand's cities in the 1920s and 1930s, so spread the rose in general and Floribundas in particular.

Prior to 1930, the spread of roses within the gardens of rural New Zealand's small farming pioneers was matched in the urban landscape through the phenomenon of suburban drift. This has continued in all the main urban centres since the 1920s, and subsequently in rural service towns, and the privately gardened landscape is now the most common urban view in New Zealand. Gardens became for the first time a part of most New Zealand homes, and roses gained the opportunity to become more than a symbol. Floribundas enabled a transfer of roses' strong cultural identity into a widespread garden presence. As gardens became the most popular domestic art form in the country, roses' position as the most popular garden flower was consolidated.

The arrival of Floribundas just as gardening became accessible to the greatest number of people is an excellent example of the rose mystery. To this must also be added the timely formation of the National Rose Society, which served to promote roses just when the need was greatest, and the arrival of the Labour Government in 1935, followed shortly after by state housing and a full acceptance of the garden suburb concept by the whole country.

State houses gave gardens to everybody. New householders were given hedge plants and fruit trees, as well as garden sheds from which to work their plots. The plans and ideals of town planners were made real by the state housing programme; by 1940, 5000 new homes were being built each year, with 5000 potential new gardens around them. New Zealand had a new body of gardeners who were learning from scratch; the rose had Floribundas, frequent and abundant flowerers, consumer-friendly characters that gave a spectacular performance with little effort from the gardener. Floribundas were the ideal plant for the moment, and from the 1930s on, as suburbia replaced rural hills as New Zealand's heartland, this new rose made itself comfortable in a whole new generation of gardens.

Floribundas had already snatched an advantage by the time state housing suburbs opened up new ground for roses. By 1932 Floribundas were second only to Hybrid Teas in popularity, making up 20 per cent of catalogue listings from leading nurseries. By the time Iceberg was released, Floribundas were well established, taking up to 39 per cent of Avenue Nursery's catalogue of that year, compared with 50 per cent for Hybrid Teas, and already had a local winner in tall, predictably pink, Queen Elizabeth.

Iceberg is the epitome of Floribunda effervescence, the like of which Queen Elizabeth was unable to match, and it was this which captured gardeners' imaginations in a way no other white rose has managed to do in New Zealand. In 1964, when the New Zealand National Rose Society published the results of the first ballot of favourite roses by its members, Iceberg was the second ranked Floribunda, scoring a third of the votes of the top rose, the Hybrid Tea, Peace.

In 1970, Iceberg was the highest scoring Floribunda, just 50 points behind the most popular Hybrid Tea, while Floribundas accounted for two of the top four roses. Iceberg's performance in this poll has continued to be remarkably consistent: third overall in 1975, second in 1980, and in the top ten every year up to 1992, including first place overall three times. It has been in the top five of the Floribunda section every year since the ballot has been conducted, a performance unmatched by any other rose. Even Peace, often considered the ultimate in rose popularity, falls well short of Iceberg in this area, only making thirty-third place in 1992, having fallen behind Iceberg in points ten years earlier.

Iceberg continues to be a phenomenon in New Zealand, a rose that reflects the egalitarianism brought by depression and war, and the arrival of the suburban society. It illustrates that health and vigour were at least as important as the cleverness breeders had made of colour, and that they were essential to the continued success of roses with an entirely new generation of gardeners, who expected their plants to grow easily and abundantly.

Stars and Stripes
Vivian Ward

Mum and roses, an image immediately familiar and comfortable, and at the same time as symbolic of feminine power and the rose mystery as Botticelli's "Primavera".

"Portrait of Mrs Ethel Violet Angus", Rita Angus (Alexander Turnbull Library)

9 Peace

Among the Roman love-poets, possession
Is a rare theme. The locked and flower-hung door,
The shivering lover, are allowed. To more
Buoyant moods, the canons of expression
Gave grudging sanction. Do we, then, assume,
Finding Propertius tear-sodden and jealous,
That Cynthia was inexorably callous?
Plenty of moonlight entered that high room
Whose doors had met his Alexandrine battles;
And she, so gay a lutanist, was known
To stitch and doze a night away, alone,
Until the poet tumbled in with apples
For penitence and for her head his wreath,
Brought from a party, of wine-scented roses.
(The garland's aptness lying, one supposes,
Less in the flowers than in the thorns beneath:
Her waking could, he knew, provide his verses
With less idyllic themes.) Onto her bed
He rolled the fruit, and adorned her head;
Then gently roused her sleeping mouth to curses.
Here the conventions reassert their power:
The apples fall and bruise, the roses wither,
Touched by a sallowed moon. But there were other
Luminous nights – (even the cactus flower
Glows briefly golden, fed by spiny flesh) –
And once, as he acknowledged, all was singing:
The moonlight musical, the darkness clinging,
And she compliant to his every wish.

Note on Propertius, *Fleur Adcock*

161

New Zealand's war memorials are a utilitarian attempt to give substance to war's grief, to create glory by institutionalising it. The flower of New Zealand's wars has, since the 1914 war in northern France, been the fiercely foreign poppy, but those flowers left on the plaques and plinths each Anzac Day are from our own gardens. These are the flowers from our hearts, and here roses' ancient rituals of death become an annual rite of nationhood.

In the crematorium grounds in Christchurch this traditional floral memorial to the war dead takes another form in a special memorial rose garden, with each death marked by a standard rose. Originally, 3000 roses were planted, of 126 different varieties, making an important rose garden in its own right, but one that has a special link with roses' deepest symbolism and confirms an aspect of European spiritualism in New Zealand. Created as it was in an era when New Zealanders were questioning more than ever their place in the world, and were claiming individuality of culture apart from that offered by Britain, the Christchurch memorial garden is something of a paradox, a place that simultaneously represents our political independence, and our cultural dependence.

The cemetery can also be the rose garden: this holds true for Christianity as much as for earlier pagan religions. Here, in Hastings, the theme is used to good effect, and Christchurch too has a rose garden memorial in remembrance of war dead.

The garden was established in 1947 as the country again counted the costs of its European tie from deep in the unquestioning calm of suburban backwaters. The 1950s were a time of stolid conservatism, of consolidating the advantages of the 1920s and 1930s with the prosperity peace brought; a time when New Zealanders refused to acknowledge that they were a Pacific people and that there was no longer a glorious British Empire, a time when the quest for comfort and security was predominant.

Predictably, from among roses' numbers came a plant in harmony with popular emotions; a plant with generous blooms — perfectly formed, mellow yellow, touched with sunset pink — from a vigorous, healthy, glossy bush. Capitalising on its superbly timed arrival, it was named Peace, in one of the greatest of all marketing decisions; the rose became the time, and the rose mystery again confirmed its special affinity with people and their moods.

It is not surprising that Peace is French, the grand finale of French rose breeding that began with the passion of Josephine 150 years earlier. Francis Meilland, the creator of Peace, was, however, definitely a breeder of the next generation, whatever the traditions that fortified his inheritance from his father, Antoine. Breeding and selling roses was as much a business for Francis Meilland as it was a vocation, and he was determined to establish high professional standards of horticulture and business practice which were unusual for the time. His was a technically proficient, ordered approach; as a result, he set the pattern for the large international breeding companies of the future.

Meilland saw the future for rose breeders was in international markets, and decided to investigate the largest of them all. Early in his partnership with his father, he embarked on an exhaustive visit to the United States, where he came face to face with consumer-directed marketing, mechanisation and copyright law for the first time. Convinced of their power, he then took them back with him to Europe. Returning to France in 1936, Francis Meilland quickly invested in colour catalogues to display his roses to best effect, as he had seen rose nurseries in America do. He also began mechanising his nursery operations, and built a cool store so that his roses could be delivered in the best possible condition.

Meilland's American-prompted innovations quickly gave him a competitive edge and contributed significantly to the success of Peace in Europe, but his most influential idea was the protection of rose breeders under the law, for he saw clearly that a good breeder had one great asset: his creativity. Naturally, the traders and dealers of the European rose business, those who paid nothing to breeders while they profited from their creations, were less than impressed with Francis Meilland and his Plant Breeders' Rights. Whatever gratitude he gained from the rose trade for Peace was balanced by the animosity he attracted in his fight for legal protection for breeders.

All of this has little to do with the actual creation of Peace, for it was originally pollinated in 1935, before Francis left on his North American journey, but his professionalism is at the heart of the fantastic success that rose has had. Without question, Peace is a superb rose, with every characteristic needed to make it a success, but it was its marketing that made it popular, and then famous; marketing that sprang from Francis Meilland's American experience and launched by the inspired name given the rose by his United States agents, Conard-Pyle.

When Peace was first released in Europe in 1942, it was known as Mme A. Meilland in France, Gloria Dei in Germany, and Gioia in Italy. Budwood of the rose had been sent to the United States in 1939, but it was not released there until 1945, when Conard-Pyle decided to call it Peace, naming it so on the day Berlin fell to Allied forces, an event that signalled the end of the war in Europe. The rest, as they say, is history.

Peace's softness, abundance and delicacy made it the perfect rose for the time; as the whole world had been shaken by the war, its relevance was worldwide. In New Zealand it was first introduced as Mme A. Meilland, and it was known officially by this name for over a decade. Popularly, however, by 1948 it was Peace. By the early 1950s it was the biggest-selling rose in the country, and remained so for almost 15 years.

This was in itself quite an achievement, but its fame was much wider spread than its sales indicate, for Peace became the one rose everybody knew as well as the one almost everybody grew.

The popularity polls of the National Rose Society confirm Peace's appeal and nursery sales performance, for it continued to attract a substantial portion of votes for 50 years after its release, and stayed in the top ten Hybrid Teas until as recently as 1990. This is not a unique achievement, but in the well-informed Rose Society world, where new roses attract more attention than they would do amongst the general public, it is something of a phenomenon, as Peace was already 20 years old in New Zealand before the first poll was conducted.

Peace also proved, if that was necessary, that Hybrid Teas which had Floribunda-quality health and abundance remained the preferred rose of New Zealand. The Hybrid Tea shape, with precisely formed buds and tightly rolled, unfurling petals, had become the classic rose shape for the new breed of rose growers from the suburbs, in spite of the popularity of Floribunda utility. When Peace combined this classicism with some of the best Floribunda characteristics, such as health and vigour, this became as much a contribution to its success as its suitably serene colour.

Gardeners wanted easy-flowering, healthy roses. If they could have them with archetypal rosebud flowers, so much the better. Francis Meilland lead his fellow breeders into the mass market world with his business techniques, and by breeding Peace he presented them with a perfect example of that market's potential. Peace's combination of the best Floribunda and Hybrid Tea characteristics was also an illustration that breeding what customers wanted was as important as marketing. Efficiency and clever marketing were needed to make a rose sell well, but for real success the breeders needed to produce a rose their new large audience wanted to buy.

The Meilland approach was what was called in the 1950s 'scientific', and science was as much a theme of the period as peace. The era of the atomic bomb was also one of jet travel, rockets, and antibiotics, and in New Zealand there was great enthusiasm for scientific applications in agriculture, most dramatically seen in aerial topdressing but most influentially in farm management. To the new generation taking charge in New Zealand — a more worldly, better educated and organised generation — science was one of the tools to take them optimistically to the future, with which they could take full advantage of the wealth generated by Europe's rebuilding and the burgeoning trade for New Zealand producers.

The rose community was receptive to the new age of science as much as any group. In 1954 the Auckland nursery of Cutlers, rose specialists since 1911, began advertising its own 'Cutler Tested Roses', plants that had been trialled for local conditions at its New Lynn grounds. Further south, Massey Agricultural College had already made its attempt at some sort of research programme with roses; at the Parnell Rose Garden there was a limited rose trial underway.

The 1950s brought a burgeoning demand for roses, which, combined with the popularity of science, facilitated more activity in the rose field by the Department of Agriculture. This led to a programme of rose experiments at the Department's horticultural research stations at Levin and Avondale. Prompting this research was the spreading bureaucracy that was rapidly increasing its involvement in every aspect of New Zealand life, and which in the agriculture sector had extended beyond providing advice to commercial horticulture into the private garden. The experiments began in 1956, under the direction of J. P. Salinger of the Horticulture Division in Wellington, a rose enthusiast who, as a horticultural advisory officer for ornamentals, was often involved in the activities of the New Zealand National Rose Society.

The subjects of the experiments were mainly of value to the nursery industry, rather than home gardeners, with their concentration on the root stocks used by nurseries to graft the buds of their different ranges of rose varieties. However, the Department did initially undertake research into the control of diseases and pests in New Zealand, which could have been of value to private rose growers, especially on

Begun in the 1930s, by the late 1940s state housing was charging ahead in anticipation of a flush of post-war prosperity — more houses, more gardens, more gardeners, more roses.
(Alexander Turnbull Library)

the problem of dieback, which had emerged shortly after the First World War and was causing some anxious moments amongst rose growers unsure of its cause.

These experiments seem to have been of little practical value to gardeners in the long term, in spite of regular reports in Rose Society publications, and they were ultimately discontinued by the Department. It was an episode that has more value as an illustration of just how involved government bureaucracy had become in ordering private life in New Zealand during the 1950s than it was as a contribution to rose gardening. Not only was the government active in developing garden suburbs through the activities of the state housing bureaucracy, it was also taking a hand in directing how the gardens should be efficiently maintained!

Specific research on the purely ornamental rose plant also serves to confirm the popularity of roses at this time, indicating that the cultural aspects of the rose, in literature and popular music, as well as its long presence in domestic art, were being transferred into garden roses as more people acquired their own sections of land. As Centifolias had once been the realisation of a myth, so too were the suburban rose gardens of the 1950s that allowed many people to make close contact with this flower, which had for so long been a symbol but was rarely real.

The suburbs, which had made such a positive beginning before the war, surged ahead in the prosperous 1950s and 1960s. In 1936, seven out of every ten New Zealanders lived in towns and cities; by 1956, this had grown to almost seven-and-a-half of every ten. By 1966 it was eight, and by 1991, there were eight-and-a-half urban dwellers for every one-and-a-half that lived in the country. Almost all of this growth was in new suburbs, which divided cityscapes into home-blocks, complete with garden, in the accepted package adopted by the State Advances Corporation in 1935. In the major cities in 1980, over 80 per cent of the population lived in what were once called 'garden suburbs', a ring of garden-bordered houses fanning out from the city centre. New fringe cities with previously unheard names like Waitakere, Manukau and Porirua were by the 1980s amongst the largest in the country, cities which had grown from new suburbs.

Roses were well placed to benefit as the suburban growth spurt gained momentum. As families without any garden traditions of their own were sucked into the suburban idyll, flowers such as roses, with a reputation outside the garden community, were taken up by these new-comers.

Although the place of roses in New Zealand gardens was well established by 1945, the rapid increase in sales of rose plants in the quarter-century that followed owes much to other established rose images. The deeply ingrained rose imagery of English literature, as well as the sentimental use of roses as an icon of love in domestic art, an image which reached a peak in late Victorian and Edwardian times, was certainly influential on a generation that had grown up with such symbols.

The expanding field of popular media advertising also carried roses well beyond the garden sphere, so that new suburban dwellers embarking on gardening for the first time had an accumulation of rose images guiding them in the strange world of plants and fertiliser. There was the example of public rose gardens as well, as those gardens built throughout the country prior to the Second World War provided a more plausible guide to what was possible in the private flower garden than did the expansive landscape collections of botanic gardens, complete with Latin name tags.

In many cases this widespread public relations activity was not enough to convince new gardeners to plant roses, especially amongst those who saw their state house sections as an opportunity for the far more functional produce of a vegetable garden. This attitude was quite widespread in the early suburban period, when potatoes were preferable to flowers of any kind. Roses' prestigious garden image, however, garnered from years in private and government gardens, combined with their intrinsic glamour to ensure that as soon as prosperity allowed it, roses quickly found a place in every suburban garden that sought to impress.

Nurseries were naturally inclined to promote rose growing to these newcomers for a number of reasons, but predominantly because the rose market was a sustainable one. People who bought roses often became entranced by the whole culture of rose growing, the opportunity for collecting, the excitement of new varieties, as well as the nuances of rose mythology. Sometimes it was the enthusiasm of particular nurserymen, people like Frank Mason, who grew and sold roses because they loved them as much as their customers' did, which attracted newcomers to the rose community. Whatever the reason, buyers of roses who became keen also became regular customers.

Post-war rose business in New Zealand had this duality of rose establishment and newcomers, and the rose Peace was as ideally suited to this situation as it was brilliantly marketed to the post-war desire for tranquillity. Its soft yellow colour, touched at the edges with rosy pink, was the culmination of a colour fashion that had begun when Hay and Lippiatt were in their prime during the early 1900s, when Pernet-Ducher first put the golden yellow into Hybrid Teas. Roses like Dickson's Lady Margaret Stewart, and McGredy's The Queen Alexandra, both of which had sold well in New Zealand, were successful early signs of the rising fashion for yellow and red/pink colour combinations.

The pre-war fashion for yellow/pink roses was promoted by the rose establishment to new customers who arrived in the 1940s and 1950s. Shot Silk, a pink/yellow bicolour of sorts, but without the subtlety or glow of Peace, was a natural attraction for visitors to the Parnell Rose Garden in 1946, the year it won its favoured rose title.

The fashion colour of the 1920s and 1930s, yellow, was superseded in the 1950s by the yellow and red/pink combinations. But by the end of the decade even this particular fashion was losing ground, in spite of the outstanding success of Peace. It seems that the great rose was a fashion peak, not a beginning, and Peace did not stimulate a torrent of new yellow/pink bicolours. Pink, of course, persevered, so that by 1960 it had stronger support amongst rose growers than it had had in 1900. The high fashion ground in rose colour, however, had been seized by the virtuoso colour performances produced by a group of new rose-breeding stars who were taking centre stage.

It seems that as the 1950s progressed, colours grew in intensity and in spectacular variety. No longer were there just journeyman reds with crimson interludes, accompanied by a sprinkling of white and simple yellows, with an honest body of pinks. Crimsons were coming back, this time as a serious colour option amongst Floribundas, rather than as a fault, as had been their earlier inclination in so many red Hybrid Perpetuals. Whites had gained some ground, actually showing a little adventure by appearing in the bicolour range for the first time, and the oranges and their fiery scarlet relatives had made a considerable advance.

These improvements in established colours were only part of the excitement, as the 1950s brought out the first of a number of new colour creations that offered completely new possibilities to rose growers. The so-called blues made their controversial entrée; coffee/tan hues became an option for the first time; as did the flashing brightness and sensational changing colours of Masquerade. This was really a novelty rose, producing blooms that moved from bright yellow buds, through pink to orange and a deep red finale.

These colours gave energy to the wonderfully vigorous contributions of Floribundas, and the newer, healthier strains of Hybrid Teas ensured that they were in demand. The results of breeders' retrospective searching were also coming to the fore, and hybrids of ancient species were added to the range of options available to New Zealand gardeners for the first time since Albertine had trumpeted the values of *R. wichuraiana* in 1921. Suddenly there were new varieties like *R. Kordesii* as well as new hybrids of Moss, Gallica, Rubignosa and Pimpinellifolia in the nursery catalogues, each with their own particular idiosyncrasies and characteristics to expand even further the already amazing variety of roses on offer.

It was a period in which roses and other domestic features of New Zealand life reflected an enthusiasm that was missing from wider political, commercial and social spheres. If there was any single public mood during the 1950s it was rampant conservatism, in itself no bad thing for roses, which have always had the ability to offer a spectacular show of passion without alienating their establishment image. If anything, the new brightness of roses offered a private alternative to the dour public landscape, and as post-war prosperity was dispersed through the country, homes and gardens became more sumptuous and more decorative.

Even as the suburbs swelled, prosperity came from new land broken in earlier in the century, which was producing for international markets returning high prices for meat, butter and wool. Making money was easy, living was easy, and the rural community claimed credit for the country's good luck, much as they had blamed others for the 'bad luck' low prices that had brought in the Depression. The 'backbone of the country' myth so popular with farmers found hearty support at this time, justifying its revival after Depression damage. It is one of New Zealand's most enduring litanies, founded in the vested interest of high country wool growers last century, and sustained by successive rural generations as a self-righteous justification for almost any preferential consideration they feel they need. Its influence can be found in many of the measures, sensible and otherwise, in which governments indulge the rural sector, and rural optimism in the 1950s sponsored some of the more bizarre instances of farming paranoia finding bureaucratic form. The outlawing of one of New Zealand's oldest roses, Sweet Briar, is one example.

Sweet Briar was never really a garden rose, but a means of fortification, and its use in hedges during the colonial period was popular and widespread. Like many other introduced plants, it flourished under New Zealand conditions and often spread to places where it was not welcome. Sweet Briar has a particular fondness for the dry South Island hill country, which is also a favourite area for large-scale sheep farming, and so came into conflict with the interests of one of the most influential colonial groups, the sheep farming station owners.

This group had wealth and considerable political power in colonial New Zealand, and their lobbying saw Sweet Briar listed as one of only five specific plants outlawed in the Noxious Weeds Act of 1900, plants which were to be eradicated throughout the country. A drastic measure indeed for a rose that is only a problem in the dry areas of the South Island and the lower east coast of the North Island, a specific problem that the Act made allowance for by creating Noxious Weed Boards in the various counties. These Boards were able to add to the Noxious Weeds Act's list of five a schedule of plants that posed problems specific to their own areas, so addressing regional variations such as those of Sweet Briar while permitting them to continue to be planted in areas where their habit was of no concern.

The inclusion of Sweet Briar in the 1900 Act is a measure of the strength of the sheep station lobby at the time, a lobby which continued to be aroused on this particular matter periodically for the next 60-odd years. The 1950s were one of those periods, a flexing of farmer muscles at a problem that had not been solved by enacting a law, and which continued to defy all attempts at a solution. Sweet Briar is tough and almost impossible to eradicate, and it became a considerable irritation to high country farmers, although its preference for roadsides and dry stream beds suggests it was less of a problem than the farmers' cries of anguish indicated. This did not prevent widespread clamour for an end to Sweet Briar.

In 1934, a memo to the Minister of Agriculture quoted the M.P. responsible for Maniototo as predicting: '...that in ten or fifteen years we shall not be able to secure tenants for our high country, as the cost of eradicating the weed [Sweet Briar] will then be prohibitive.' It appears that in spite of attempts ranging from flame throwers to the most poisonous sprays available, Sweet Briar continued to flourish, especially after the rabbit population was drastically reduced. Rabbits had kept the roses under control by eating new growth and young plants, and gave a clear sign as early as 1936 that by grazing there was a way of managing the problem. By 1955 this had not yet dawned on the farming community, and in that year the Otago branch of Federated Farmers was

The rose continued to be a persistent motif in design, changing to suit contemporary style. This example is from the famous art deco Rothmans building in Napier.

moved to suggest the introduction of an insect pest that attacked roses. In writing to the Secretary of the D.S.I.R. on the matter, the Secretary of the branch, Mr C. A. Monroe, suggested that the problem such an insect would cause to domestic rose growers could be deferred by using insecticides to protect their plants.

This approach was confirmed by a resolution of the Annual Conference of Federated Farmers in 1956, and in relaying this to the Minister of Agriculture, the General Secretary of the Federation went so far as to say that '...the consequences [of not destroying Sweet Briar] might be disastrous to the national economy.' Quite an overstatement considering the land at risk was so marginally productive it was un-economic to effectively spray with the appropriate weedkillers that had become available a few years earlier. Luckily, the Minister of Agriculture, K. J. Holyoake, whose brother was a leading rosarian who also served as President of the New Zealand National Rose Society, acknowledged some of the positive aspects of agricultural protection by rejecting the introduction of a rose parasite, and saved rose growers from what could have been for them a disastrous mistake.

By the end of the 1950s, improvement in the management of low-rainfall tussock areas of the South Island in particular, and generally improved pasture management, were shown to control Sweet Briar effectively on productive land, and the ruckus subsequently died down. Although a disaster for the mostly urban rose community was averted, and rampant Sweet Briar in the high country was subsequently brought under control, this most attractive and historic plant remains an outlaw in a country where it should be revered.

Matangi
Vivian Ward

The modern love goddess and the rose.
"Marilyn", Bert Stern

10 Commerce

I recall, only minutes ago, a dying rose released five of its petals all in one go, drawing attention like a magnet to their cushioned fall. A hushed achievement. No fanfare or regret. And no flowers, please.

I am thinking of marketing, Fallen Rose-Petal Tea

Smiles like flowers come and go, *Hone Tuwhare*

The 1950s were an introduction to the promising flourish of New Zealand's own rose identity, and from the 1960s came the individuals whose commercial skills transformed rose growing into a modern industry capable of realising that identity. The innovations of post-war breeders in Europe and the United States gave a stimulus to the rose trade, secured by business expertise. This gave a lead to New Zealand rose growers, and, with the burgeoning of suburbs, for the first time New Zealand had a nursery trade large enough to encourage specialisation. Nurseries that preferred growing roses to other aspects of their business were able to concentrate on their favourite plants, without sacrificing business prospects. After years of following in the wake of European developments, New Zealand's rose community was starting to take the initiative.

As always, it was the efforts of individuals that changed directions and by example led the rose industry into new areas. Shortly before 1950, 13-year-old Laurie Bell indulged his interest in roses by teaching himself to bud. Rose budding was more than a little unusual for a teenage boy in a country where rugby, not roses, was the prevailing passion. But Laurie was absorbed by his dreams of a huge rose garden even then. At 16, his mind still full of roses, Mr Bell senior wisely decided to encourage his son by arranging a loan from the building society so that young Laurie could buy two acres in Glen Eden and begin growing his own roses. Not only did the roses sold off that small block repay the loan on time, Laurie also secured another two acres in nearby Sunnyvale to expand his rose gardens. By the time he began his nurseryman's apprenticeship at nearby Palmers, Laurie already had experience well beyond his years and he continued his roses as a sideline during his training.

Laurie Bell's West Auckland neighbourhood was the home of a number of leading rose nurseries, some of the largest and most successful in the country. As well as Palmers, who were growing some 10,000 rose plants each year during Laurie's time with them, the old firm of Cutlers at New Lynn had a nationwide reputation and an extensive list of mail-order customers for their rose plants. As if this were not enough, the Baldwin nursery at Glen Eden was one of the most progressive and dynamic rose nurseries around. George Baldwin had returned from the war determined to make his interest in roses pay, and he became one of the first to commit his whole business to roses. The 30,000 plants he grew gave substance to Laurie Bell's best dreams of paddocks full of flowering rose plants in a large expansive nursery, and George Baldwin became a mentor of considerable influence to the young nurseryman who saw his own future lined with masses of roses.

In 1958, with Laurie Bell still a young 25-year-old, but already with the experience of 12 years' rose growing, his own company, Bell Roses, opened for business in Henderson. Laurie wanted to be the biggest and the best in the country, and to do that required an extensive mail list, for the rose business was a mail-order business, with customers in every town in New Zealand. This was a pattern of trade that had evolved over more than 100 years of nursery business, with customers sending for catalogues from the specialists and then ordering direct from the experts in every field of garden and orchard plants.

Bell Roses immediately set about rapidly enlarging the list of customers Laurie already had from his part-time business, and shortly after they opened their doors the demise of George Baldwin gave the new

LEFT: Laurie Bell, the big rose gardener full of bright ideas and the energy to make them work. RIGHT: Bell Roses' first home in Henderson, with an early order of container roses on its way to Foodtown.

company a lucky break. After the break-up of his marriage, George Baldwin decided to sell up; he sold his extensive mail-order list to Bell Roses, and then compounded this valuable contribution by offering to work with Laurie while he got his business up to speed. George Baldwin's contribution may not have been essential to the phenomenal success of Laurie Bell's company, but his years of support for Laurie, and the commercial value of his knowledge and his customers, brought that success far earlier than might otherwise have been expected.

Laurie Bell had opened as the mail-order business for roses was reaching its peak, and the marketing techniques Bell's adopted were more sophisticated than any in New Zealand at the time. As well as the sales centre in Great North Road, Henderson, which was open on Saturdays even in 1960, customers could write or telephone Bell's from anywhere in the country. The catalogues, complete with colour photographs of the most likely roses of the year, included a range of ancillary items such as gift tokens, proprietary rose fertiliser and spray, trellises, frames and archways for the garden, rose labels and markers, stakes and secateurs, expanding the selling of plants into a multi-level service for rose gardeners. The selection Bell's offered, and its smart presentation, predicted the arrival of garden centres and the ultimate demise of mail order as the principal means of selling roses in New Zealand. Bell Roses was the beginning of the end for the old rose trade.

In the meantime, the huge rose nursery of Laurie Bell's dreams quickly became a reality, for Bell's soon became the largest rose growers in the country, selling more than three times the number of roses that had impressed Laurie in Baldwin's nursery less than ten years earlier. By 1966, Bell's were growing over 400,000 roses a year, of 362 different varieties, and virtually all were current releases from the great breeding houses. Bell's catalogues contained information on rose gardening, including a calendar of spraying, fertilising and pruning activities, as well as providing tips on suitable designs for gardens with roses. They were rose growing handbooks as well as sales catalogues, and sold the whole idea of roses as much as they offered a selection of individual plants for sale.

Some of the techniques of the catalogues from the old days were retained, especially the idea of making available collections of roses with particular characteristics, or functions, suitable for new gardeners. In 1966 there were six collections in the Bell Roses catalogue, each of six roses: top Hybrid Teas (without Peace); top standards; 'All-Time Favourites'; a fragrant collection; top Floribundas; and climbers. By 1972, when the impact of garden centres was being felt, it would seem that this technique was still working well, as the range had expanded to nine collections. Bell's, however, suffered a dramatic decline in business as mail order rapidly gave way to the new force in the garden market-place, the garden centre. By this time the nursery was producing less than half what it was during the peak of mail-order sales, and like the rest of the nursery industry Laurie Bell had to address the need for change if he wanted his business to survive.

Garden centres were a product of urban growth and the drive for efficiency through standardisation, a process that replaced small independent specialist retailers with large stores. Self-service was promoted as being preferable to the personal service offered by traditional retailers, and display and design expertise superseded product knowledge as the means of success in retailing. Supermarkets and suburban shopping centres established the trend; garden centres were a logical extension of it, making specialist rose knowledge less important than pretty displays when it came to selling roses.

As garden centres, strategically placed in the suburbs that wanted their wares most, burgeoned, nurseries had to decide whether to become suppliers to the new centres or set up in opposition. Those, like Bell Roses, who wished to preserve the success they had achieved under the old system, became suppliers and modified their businesses accordingly. The others concentrated on their specialist rose customers, those who wanted more service and attention than was available in the impersonal garden centres and supermarkets. Both did well when they adapted their businesses to suit the needs of their specific market, but the adaptation required quite a change to the established approach of growing and selling roses.

This change was not only at the sales end but also in the way nurseries were managed and their plants grown. Garden centres were display-oriented, and the bare root plants that rose nurseries had always sold and shipped to their customers did not have any visual appeal at all. Garden centre customers, unlike those who bought on the strength of a pretty picture in a catalogue, were attracted by healthy, smart-looking plants, preferably with flowers on them. They also wanted to be able to walk into a garden centre, buy what they liked the look of and take it home to plant immediately. No longer could plants be dispatched at specific times of the year that were suitable for planting, as the customers were not prepared to wait. Garden centre customers wanted container-grown roses that looked good.

Rose nurseries had refined their production techniques to suit the mail-order business. Buds of new rose varieties arrived by mail from Europe, carefully packed in moss. After being acclimatised here, the buds would be taken off and budded onto another rose plant with healthy roots, which would keep the rose vigorous throughout its life. For many years the most popular rootstock in New Zealand was a local version of the Monetti rose, developed by W. E. Lippiatt and known as Lippiatt's Monetti. But with that stock a favourite of the introduced grass grub, by the 1950s it was superseded, predominantly by *R. multiflora*, as well as a number of others, of which *R. indica major* is the most important.

Approximately 18 months after the buds arrived, the first of the new rose varieties were ready for sale. They were pulled from the ground in which they were growing, and packed for shipment in June and July to their new garden homes. Invariably, these plants were ordered well in advance, and had to be planted as soon as they arrived. In the bigger nurseries, the pulling of roses was done mechanically, and the spraying and maintenance of the nursery plants was also fully mechanised. This system had to be changed to meet the growing demand for container roses.

There was another pressure brought to bear by the arrival of garden centres, one that demanded from the nurseries greater efficiency and mechanisation than ever before: there was now less profit in every rose plant. No longer was the nursery dealing directly with the rose gardener; a middle man meant the new plants had to be competitive in a more competitive market.

The new business environment demanded that efficiency be addressed everywhere within the nursery operation. Air freight made importing budwood less of a risk; the introduction of new budding tech-niques and importing highly skilled, fast and efficient budding teams from Europe and North America vastly improved the efficiency of some nurseries. It is not surprising that Bell Roses has been an industry leader in all these areas, as it was in the development of the production of con-tainer-grown roses. In the use of imported budding teams alone, the improvement in productivity of a nursery is remarkable. Before their introduction to New Zealand, local budders at their best were capable of processing 1000 buds each day, of which some 80 per cent would successfully take. The imported teams are turning out 4000, with a success rate over 90 per cent, in the same time.

Woman and rose again, this time in the hands of a leading New Zealand artist, Rita
Angus, who was one of the pioneers of modern painting here.
"Figure with Rose", Rita Angus (Alexander Turnbull Library)

FOLLOWING PAGES: John Reynolds, one of New Zealand's finest contemporary artists,
makes his response to William Blake's famous poem – another artist is drawn by
the rose mystery.
"The Sick Rose", John Reynolds

R EYNOLDS 1991

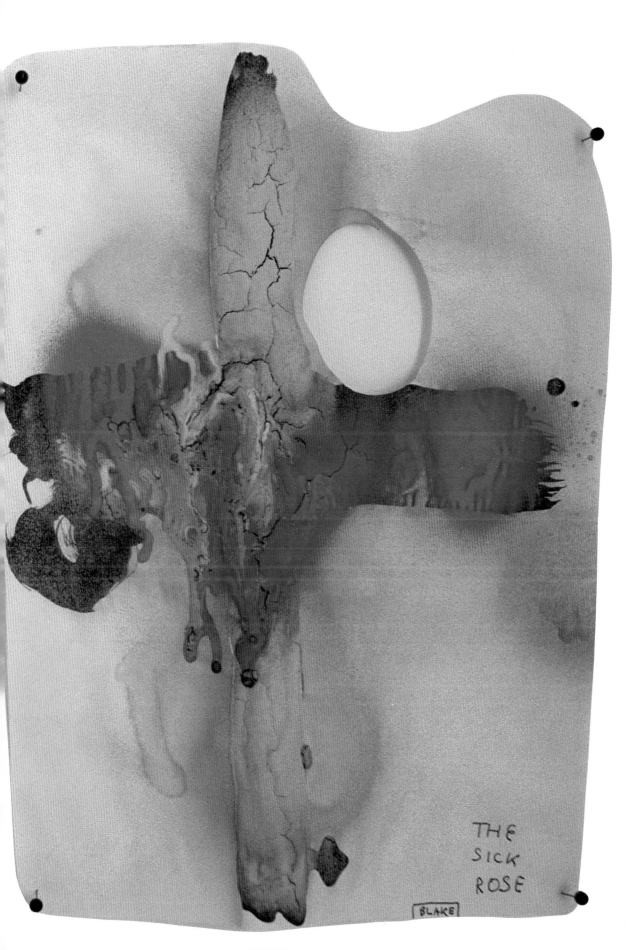

THE
SICK
ROSE

BLAKE

Not surprisingly for an artist who often works with ideas of sexuality, Fiona
Pardington frequently uses roses, and here the body and the rose are the same
– interchangeable, obvious and yet mysterious.
"Soft Target", Fiona Pardington

Garden centres also required a change in the marketing strategies of the specialist rose nurseries, one that had less to do with the plants they sold and more with the way they promoted themselves. While it was important the nurseries selling to garden centres formed good relations with the plant buyers, it was also important that their brands were well enough known by the customers to prompt them to buy. This self-promotion remains an area that the rose growers in New Zealand have still not come to grips with, but the promotion of rose breeders in New Zealand from the early 1960s has served to do at least half the job and has made an important contribution to the creation of a New Zealand rose breeding industry.

Avenue Nurseries, established by Phil Gardener in Levin during the mid 1950s, was a leader in the promotion of Europe's foremost rose breeders of the day. Gardener was completing his Master of Science degree during the early Avenue days, and his scientific sensitivities were as evident in the degree of credit he gave each of the breeders of the roses he listed, as they were in his offerings of the latest species hybrids. Other than W. E. Lippiatt, who had an interest as a breeder himself, the degree of credit given to breeders by Avenue Nurseries was unique in New Zealand, and it established early support for breeders in one of the most controversial issues of the international rose community: breeders' rights.

The European battle between nurseries and breeders was one of branding, and while it was a new concept to Europeans until it was introduced to them by Francis Meilland, it is one that has been a feature of all successful international products during the past 50 years. Distributors of most internationally recognised products acknowledge the power of the brand name in their marketing, and pay the originator for the advantage this gives them. Just as Chanel has a cachet in the perfume trade, Yves St Laurent in the fashion business, Moet et Chandon with wine, so too do Coca Cola, McDonald's, Levis, and any number of other products, and for each a royalty is paid from sales. What Meilland wanted was similar branding of his roses, and a well monitored system of royalties for his, and others', new roses. A Meilland, Tantau, Kordes, Poulsen or McGredy rose, he believed, was their respective intellectual, or creative, property, and remained so, no matter how many nurseries produced their own plants of each variety.

As rose marketing became more sophisticated the importance of this issue increased, particularly as rose markets became better organised and more diverse, and nurseries lost their direct influence on their customers' preferences. For many, the selling of a rose with a reputation like Peace focused attention, not only on the integrity of Meilland's claim, but also on the potential of marketing a name, or a brand, with international respectability. The attitude of Avenue Nurseries — to promote the name of the breeders alongside their roses — prepared New Zealand rosarians for a role in the international rose trade, simply by making New Zealanders comfortable with the concept of breeder primacy in the creation of famous roses.

Avenue was New Zealand agent for many of the rose breeding avant-garde who made an incredible impact during the 1960s. With McGredy, Kordes, Tantau and Jackson & Perkins in the stable of breeders whose roses it offered, Avenue presented a glittering range of the latest and the best to its customers. Bell's, too, had formed a relationship with a leading international breeder, American Ralph Moore, whose agency they acquired in 1961. This was in response to another of Laurie Bell's ideas, as innovative as that which had made him the owner of the largest rose nursery in the country. This time, however, Laurie was thinking small, for Ralph Moore was the world's leading breeder of Miniature roses. It was an idea that would give Bell Roses another big commercial success as the local rose market continued to change.

From the very beginning, Bell Roses had a good selection of Miniatures, a rose family with a long history but which was not given much consideration in New Zealand by serious rose growers and even less by rose nurseries. This is an unfortunate omission, as the first rose in New Zealand, the pretty little Crimson China of Ruatara, was, in character at least, the first miniature rose, a small hardy plant that grew happily in a tiny pot and pushed out regular bursts of colour through-out most of the year. A number of China roses, of the *R. chinensis minima* family, were popular as miniature curiosities during the early 1800s, but they virtually disappeared from catalogues for 60 years until they were rediscovered in Switzerland around 1918. By the 1920s they were again enjoying a rush of popularity, and also attracted the attention of a number of breeders, with the Spaniard, Pedro Dot Martinez, having considerable success with them in the 1930s.

By the 1950s a Dutchman, Jan de Vink, had also made a name for himself with some interesting Miniatures (after more than 20 years of breeding), by which time Ralph Moore was also attracting attention with Miniatures like Little Buckaroo. By 1960, Ralph Moore was specialising entirely in Miniatures, and with his own interest in the smallest of roses it was appropriate that Laurie Bell should contact Moore to establish one of the longest-held rose agency relationships in New Zealand.

Miniatures appealed in New Zealand in much the same way as Floribundas had, through the changing demands of new rose customers. Small roses, especially those grown in containers, gave city-dwelling rose enthusiasts without the benefit of large gardens an opportunity to indulge their interest. As more and more varieties were released, they even found favour with specialist rose growers who did not have a space problem. Miniatures' portability and the perfect, tiny form of their flowers made them ideal for collecting, and as garden design became more popular, Miniatures filled a need for those whose gardens were not organised to accommodate the haphazard collection of new and inter-esting plants. All the collector of Miniatures needs is a verandah, patio, or similar little space away from the order of a proper garden, or the restrictions of life in a city flat.

Garden centres also gave Miniatures, which had a lot of visual appeal, a boost. The charm of Miniature roses undermined the pre-conceptions of rose gardeners, as well as attracting the attention of those who had never previously considered roses at all. Bell Roses had already

Sixties architecture, along with more concrete and space for cars, still had room for roses.

recognised the persuasive powers of Miniatures on display, and during the mid 1960s introduced roses to supermarkets for the first time, a sales area that grew slowly but has become an important outlet for Miniatures.

Miniatures and garden centres almost go hand-in-hand: it is unlikely these pretty little roses would have sold so well had mail order continued, and their appeal to general customers makes them an attractive proposition to garden centre operators. Certainly, Laurie Bell had picked another winner when he latched on to them, for sales of Miniatures have come to equal that of all other roses in New Zealand, with an estimated 1.5 million plants sold annually during the early 1990s. That is a substantial number in a country with only 3 million people, and an incredible surge in popularity unmatched by any other rose type since Hybrid Perpetuals blazed around the world.

By the time the 1980s arrived, Bell Roses had reclaimed the rose sales they had lost during the 1960s and relocated from Henderson to a new, larger site on Hobsonville Road, Waitakere, where Laurie Bell and his family continue to run the largest rose growing business in the country. As well as holding a substantial portion of the garden rose market in full-size roses, the company also supplies almost 90 per cent of the Miniature roses in New Zealand. It continues to release the latest Miniature offerings from Ralph Moore, as well as a range from the giant French company Delbard. Since 1960 Bell's has also acquired a new neighbour, one who has been as influential in the development of another area of the rose business as Bell's has been with Miniatures. Frank Schuurman arrived in New Zealand from the Netherlands in 1963, a young man with experience in rose growing and an inclination to use that experience to set himself up in his adopted country. There could not have been a greater contrast between Frank Schuurman's old and new homes than that between the respective rose industries. In the district of Aalsmeer, south of Amsterdam, there is the largest concentration of commercial rose growers in the world, all growing stems for the massive Dutch cut flower industry, which now supplies approximately 1000 million roses each year for the international flower market. New Zealand in 1963 had few commercial cut rose growers, and the cut flower business was supplied with roses by garden rose nurseries who took flowers from their year-old plants and sold them for an ancillary income.

Shortly after setting up home in west Auckland, and after working with one of the cut rose pioneers here, fellow Dutch immigrant, Walter van Lier, Frank Schuurman established his own rose growing operation not far from Bell Roses in Henderson. Utilising all his Dutch experience, Schuurman quickly built Sunbeam Roses into an important rose growing business, one with an eye on the developing cut flower market in New Zealand. Early on he imported cut flower rose varieties from the Netherlands, which he supplied to the new rose growers who also saw considerable opportunity in this expanding business, at the same time steadily increasing his own cut flower growing and building a healthy trade in garden roses.

In 1972, on the arrival of New Zealand's first rose maestro, Sam McGredy, Frank facilitated the establishment of a McGredy breeding house in Henderson by offering Sam a glasshouse for rent. It became the first home of the famous McGredy roses in New Zealand, and Frank Schuurman's relationship with the great rose breeder during the decade and more he operated from Sunbeam was enough inspiration for him to begin his own breeding, a step that was to produce considerable international success with the cut rose variety, Darling.

Darling is a sport of the remarkably successful Meilland rose, Sonia, a delightful blend of pinks that has since 1975 produced more cut flowers in Europe than any other rose. Darling was not the result of an intentional breeding programme but it served to illustrate the potential of the cut flower business for new roses. In the Netherlands alone over 1 million plants of Darling, originally known as Cream Delight, have been sold, and Frank Schuurman is now actively working on his own breeding programme, aimed at making a breakthrough in the most modern areas: spray roses for the cut flower industry, a type steadily growing in popularity, and the flourishing Miniature, Patio and Ground Cover roses.

It seems another piece of rose mystery that Frank Schuurman's name as a New Zealand breeder should have been introduced by the colour pink. Darling's parent is probably the greatest of all cut flower pinks, and the delightful Tinkerbell, a fragrant, soft pink Spray rose has already won many converts since its release through the garden centres in the early 1990s. As if to underline the pink influence, a sweetly pink Schuurman Patio rose, Little Opal, won the 1992 Rose Introducers of New Zealand Rose of the Year Award for the Champion Rose in the Auckland Botanical Gardens trial ground.

With around 12 million rose stems now being produced by New Zealand's cut rose growers annually, and exports worth around $1.5 million, this section of the rose community has obviously become an important one, not yet as large or as visible as the garden rose section but no longer the parasite it once was. If Frank Schuurman's breeding success continues, the value of cut flower roses could be far greater than New Zealand's potential to grow and supply flowers for overseas markets, becoming an export of inspiration as influential to other rose communities as the imports from European and American breeders have been to New Zealand's.

The rose industry that has emerged in New Zealand is a significant one, with both the garden flower and cut flower sections active, and each is made up mostly of efficient, highly technical businesses. Nurseries throughout the country supply rose plants to the large garden centre trade, as well as to the cut flower growers, and the small, but still active, mail-order business that continues to attract rose specialists looking for an affinity between themselves and their rose suppliers. It is a long way from the fruit trees, Sweet Briar and vegetable suppliers of colonial New Zealand, who had a small and steady trade in Hybrid Perpetuals while Queen Victoria still ruled, but it is a business W. E. Lippiatt would have understood, especially its respect for the breeders who give it energy.

Darling
Vivian Ward

11 Inspiration

Sam McGredy would have been welcome in New Zealand for his conviviality and his enthusiasm, even if he had not brought his famous rose breeding operation with him. But he did, and in doing so he took advantage of New Zealand's abundance to produce his greatest roses. In return he gave a transforming energy to the New Zealand rose community, as well as an instant reputation as a new and exciting source of remarkable roses.

For almost 160 years, the New Zealand rose was an elusive thing, a colonist with its source and inspiration European. So too were those who nurtured it here, those who took the steady stream of fine and forgettable roses that travelled out to New Zealand from the great European breeding houses and acclimatised them to New Zealand's growing and social conditions. Like their plants, they were also immigrants, wanderers whose roots and traditions were European, but whose home of choice was New Zealand.

Here they thrived in an environment as fertile as that which encouraged their roses and their businesses. Both the Lippiatts, father and son, were born in England, and the garden techniques and attitudes passed from one to the other, particularly the special fondness for roses, were English. Similarly, it was his own experiences of cultivating florists' roses in his Dutch homeland that gave Frank Schuurman the understanding and expertise with which he energised New Zealand's cut rose industry.

Although these immigrants became New Zealanders, often with greater patriotic zeal than their indigenous neighbours, and the roses they bred were New Zealand roses, the predominant influences on them were external. The lead each gave to the local rose community was an extension of their European experience, and was developed through their continued contact with the European rose industry. It was a contact which in W. E. Lippiatt's case acknowledged the importance of individual rose breeders, and established a breeder-friendly rose tradition, one that made it easy to include an established talent like McGredy.

What Sam McGredy in his turn did was to move New Zealand from the periphery of the rose world into the centre. By making it the base for his rose breeding programme he put New Zealand's name alongside a virtuoso breeding performance which must rank as one of the greatest in rose history. If there is a climax to the rose mystery's remarkable New Zealand story, it is the antipodean career of Sam McGredy.

Sam McGredy, son of Sam McGredy III, a man whose pedigree is one of the most illustrious in the rose world, never intended to become a rose breeder. His father died when he was only two, and the famous nursery and breeding house near Portadown in Northern Ireland was managed by Sam's uncle, Walter Johnston, on the understanding that young Sam would take over when he was old enough.

Sam, it seems, never considered the possibility, but proceeded through his schooling and brief university career with the intention of enjoying every moment, and the hope of one day becoming a journalist. By the time he arrived at the family nursery ready for work in 1952, he was an intelligent young man, skilled in partying and the finer points of rugby, but hardly prepared to take up the rose breeding reputation created by his forbears. He was terrified by his new responsibility, and shocked by the poor state of the nursery's breeding house after years of neglect, but decided to attack the problems with all his considerable vigour. It was the sort of decisive action that became a feature of the outstanding breeding career that followed, and ultimately lead to his emigration to New Zealand.

Once he had decided to take on rose breeding, Sam determined that if he was going to do it, he was going to be the best, good enough at least to match the performances of his father and grandfather. There was no doubt more than a touch of naivety in his decision, for he hardly knew what he was taking on and other than his name, enthusiasm, and a shared breeding house, Sam had inherited nothing from the house of McGredy. To make it work he had to replace everything and start again, with new parent plants, with new techniques, new equipment and a new vision on which to focus his enormous talent.

In 1954 the first parents of roses from the fourth Sam McGredy generation were sown, the beginning of what is the long and risky business of hybridising. Because the plants at the beginning of this process are themselves hybrids, each containing a genetic cocktail according to its own heredity, no breeder is entirely sure what will come of each cross. In an effort to overcome the many variables of such a process, thousands of plants are raised from each hybrid, and those likely to succeed as new roses are selected from this. Some breeders claim they raise as many as 100,000 plants for each rose considered good enough to make it to market.

Following selection, the likely plants are subjected to four years of trials and further culling before a rose has proved its worth, and can be named and promoted as a worthy example of the breeder's ability. This whole process can take as long as seven years from first pollination to release, so Sam McGredy could have expected to wait until 1962 before he had roses of his own to offer, and even longer before he could have reasonably expected to produce one that would win a major prize and prove his inherited reputation.

Working with energy and speed, and the special ruthless talent for identifying class that all good artists have, Sam released his first rose, Salute, in 1958, just four years after kick-off. A year later he won his first gold medal with Orangeade; in 1961 the President's International Trophy for the top rose of the year in Britain went to Mischief. Sam McGredy had arrived like a shooting star, larger than life, vibrant, brilliantly innovative — characteristics not unlike the roses that would make his reputation as one of the finest rose breeders ever.

Under Sam, McGredy's name again became a regular feature of the winners' lists at major rose competitions around Europe, and Sam was quickly accepted by the group of young rose breeders whose creations, by the mid 1960s, were leading the rose world into a new age with their health, vigour and intense colour. Neils Poulsen, Reimer Kordes and Jan Spek were Sam McGredy's competitors, but they were also friends, and with Dickson and Tantau they made up as talented a bunch of breeders as any in rose history.

Sam McGredy was not just a breeder of exciting roses, however, he was also an astute business operator who modernised the production and marketing approach of the old family firm, and employed the most sophisticated public relations techniques, at which he has become a master. He also gave considerable thought to the wider issues concerning the rose business, particularly the critical topic of breeders' rights, in the protection of which lay the future of those rosarians whose skills lay in creating new roses. In taking up the battle for these rights, Sam was championing the cause of the artist rose breeder against that of the plant dealer.

In adopting this issue, and by modernising his own business practice as nurseryman and breeder, Sam became the British heir of Francis Meilland's philosophy. It is an association that also has links through the McGredy development of bicolour roses throughout the first half of this century, and ultimately the use of Margaret McGredy as a parent in the breeding of the most famous bicolour of all, Peace. It is perhaps a touch of rose mystery irony that Francis Meilland died in 1958, the year that Sam McGredy, rose breeder, unveiled his first creation, Salute.

In 1958 Sam had already been lobbying for breeders' rights for three years, continuing the battle begun in Britain by Francis Meilland. In 1951, Francis Meilland had attracted the fury of the French rose industry by securing a Brevet d'Invention for his rose Rouge Meilland, confirming his right in France to royalties from its sale. He compounded this by applying for trademark protection in Britain, in spite of opposition from nurserymen and the National Rose Society, pressure that ultimately ended in court, with Meilland losing.

Sam used his considerable powers of persuasion to lobby the British Government for legislation to protect the breeders, of which he and his Northern Ireland neighbours, Dicksons, were the largest. In 1964, after nine years of sometimes bitter debate, the Government passed the Plant Variety and Seeds Act. A victory for the breeders, this went most of the way towards a satisfactory conclusion, but remained as unpopular with British nurseries as Sam McGredy's roses were popular. For Sam it remains the single issue on which the continued success of the rose industry depends.

Sam McGredy began his association with New Zealand very early on in his rose breeding career, when the innovative Avenue Nurseries in Levin became his local agent. During the planning of an international rose convention for Wellington in 1961, it was decided that an international guest was needed to justify the name, and Phil Gardener of Avenue offered to contact Sam and see if he was available. With his usual enthusiasm for new projects, and new places, Sam accepted and made the long journey to this distant outpost of the rose industry. He was not here long, but long enough to form a strong bond with this green country and its friendly people.

As feature speaker at the Wellington conference at a time when overseas experts were revered in New Zealand, Sam McGredy made good use of the publicity surrounding his visit to become the best-known breeder amongst New Zealand's rose community. When he returned in 1964 for Rose Week in Auckland, he capitalised on his visit by giving one of his new releases a local name, Tiki.

Naturally for New Zealand, Tiki was a pink rose, with a soft wash of apricot; typically for McGredy, it was large and healthy, with something of the style of Hybrid Teas and the abundance of Floribundas, a type known in America (and for a time in New Zealand) as Grandiflora. The name Sam chose, Tiki, was a reflection of the instant affection he felt for things Maori, especially the Maori capacity for generosity and for their music. It is an affinity that has continued to appear in the names of many of his most famous roses, giving to this colonist plant at least a little of the colour of its new home.

Sam McGredy was enchanted by New Zealand, and not just by its Maori side, or its rugby, but also by a people he describes as essentially kind and gentle, and by a land in which roses flourish. He became a regular visitor, and while here in 1969 gave another of his roses a Maori name, this time Pania, and again it was pink. A Hybrid Tea, Pania won a gold medal at the first International Rose Trial conducted at the new trial grounds in Palmerston North, and joined Tiki amongst the popular roses in the New Zealand National Rose Society's annual poll, after being something of a star at the 1971 World Rose Convention held in Hamilton.

The 1971 convention was the first fully international rose event in New Zealand, and it attracted delegates and breeders from every major rose country in the world. It was an occasion that gave Hamilton an instant reputation as a rose city, elevated the status of New Zealand in the eyes of the international rose community, and convinced Sam McGredy that if the vicious craziness in Northern Ireland became too much for him and his family, it was to New Zealand that he would come.

On his return home, Ulster's sectarian violence had become worse. Sam McGredy again made a bold instant decision, one he has since claimed is the best he ever made. Four days after his return, he was flying back to New Zealand to discuss the problems of breeders' rights with New Zealand politicians, for it was only the lack of this protection for his work that prevented his immediate immigration.

After his experience of the ten-year-long bitter battle to have the Plant Variety and Seeds Act passed in Britain, Sam was a little anxious about the political response. He was certain he had the sort of support from the rose community that breeders' rights had not enjoyed in Britain, but he had little experience of the New Zealand politicians who were in control. All he knew was that the local system was based on that

Dublin Bay, Auckland Rose of the Year in 1993. The finest of all modern climbers? RIGHT: Sam McGredy with the Queen Mother in 1964, having just named his rose Elizabeth of Glamis after her.

of Westminster, and that was enough to cause concern if his previous experience was a measure. But he was amazed at the speed with which a meeting was arranged between him and the Minister of Agriculture, Mr Carter, and Mr Moyle, the Opposition agriculture spokesman. The meeting was short and conclusive, and Sam McGredy was soon heading back to Ireland to prepare his business and his family for their emigration to New Zealand.

Moving so far was an extreme option. Sam had to sell his large and successful nursery, cease to be a high-powered managing director of a multi-million dollar business, and become a hands on rose breeder again, something he had not done for ten years and which he was more than a little unsure about. While he was certain he would fit into New Zealand personally, he was less certain about his commercial future and even considered the possibility of retirement.

Sam McGredy left the European rose world at what seemed the peak of his powers, shortly after the release of Picasso, a dramatically coloured pink and white Floribunda with 'hand painted' red patterns on the petals. It was a sensation, a dazzling achievement that confirmed the substantial contribution of Sam McGredy to roses' most creative era. It was also, in spite of Sam's completely new start in 1955, a powerful reminder of the McGredy influence on bicolour roses, which began with The Queen Alexandra Rose in 1918. If Sam wanted to retire, he would go out at the top; but he had really just begun, and there was considerable concern that his departure for New Zealand was the end of the McGredy line.

Shortly afterwards, far from the energised headquarters of Portadown, in quiet Henderson, Sam McGredy grabbed the handles of his own wheelbarrow in a greenhouse he had leased from Frank Schuurman. He had decided to continue, not as managing director of a nursery conglomerate, or as president of the McGredy International Rose Corporation, but as a simple breeder, concentrating entirely on what he knew he did best: creating fine roses. Picasso was not an end, it was merely a new beginning — for Sam McGredy, the New Zealand rose community and the whole rose world.

At first there were a few problems to overcome with the different climate, conditions, and seasons, as well as the fact that while the McGredy breeding house was in Henderson, the seedlings were raised near his agent in Levin, so there was the problem of a 1200-kilometre round trip just to keep in touch. With the alternate seasons, the first seed brought out from Northern Ireland had to be kept in the fridge from February to August before it could be germinated, and when it did the Auckland climate set it off like punnets of sprouts for the salad bar. Just when Sam was convinced he was living in breeder's paradise, he was knocked back by a problem unknown in Portadown: downy mildew. It would take all the generous support and technical back-up the Ministry of Agriculture could provide before that particular problem was licked.

By the time the McGredy family had settled in New Zealand, the National Government of which Mr Carter was a member had lost the 1972 election and Colin Moyle was Minister of Agriculture. In spite of this, the political assurances given earlier were stuck to and Sam's decision to speak to both major parties paid dividends with the rapid introduction and passing of the Plant Varieties Act in 1973, effective from 1974.

Properly, it was a McGredy rose that was the first to be released under the control of that legislation, the holder of New Zealand Plant Breeders' Right, Number 1. Significantly, for both New Zealand and Sam McGredy, it was another in the 'painted' line that Picasso had so brilliantly proclaimed, this time with a Maori name, Matangi.

The individuals from the past who had made such invaluable contributions to New Zealand rose history had made conditions perfect for Sam McGredy to finally create, and establish, successful international rose breeding in New Zealand. Without Sam and his enormous talent, it would never have happened when it did, nor would it have been so swiftly acknowledged, but a number of individuals who preceded him made his success of national importance. W. E. Lippiatt and Frank Mason laid a strong nursery foundation of high standard; Alfred Buxton put roses firmly into a New Zealand garden design; George Baldwin advanced specialisation; Laurie Bell made roses big business; Frank Schuurman expanded the trade into new areas; and finally, Phil Gardener exposed the latest generation of great rose breeders to the New Zealand public, and made both trade and growers aware of their importance and their influence on the future.

Sam fitted into New Zealand easily and quickly, because he was an international star, and because his easy character and humour were suited to the lifestyle. His breeding activity has also slipped easily into the rose community so that Sam McGredy roses are now considered New Zealand roses as much by New Zealanders as they are by Sam himself, who is now a New Zealander by choice. In the names of his roses can be found his assimilation into New Zealand life: Nobilo's Chardonnay, Auckland Metro, Wanaka, Kapiti and, of course, Matangi.

Matangi is special. Not only was it the first to be protected under the new Act, but its substantial contribution to the hand-painted set Sam had begun with Picasso was a sign that not only was the McGredy line still going, it was flourishing and progressing. Matangi was also extremely popular, racing into the top five in the Rose Society lists, then keeping its place for ten years. In 1991/92, 18 years after its release, Matangi was still the eleventh placed Floribunda, not really surprising for a rose that has always grown very well almost everywhere in New Zealand, and which has enough class to have won the top British rose award, the President's Trophy.

The name Matangi came from a favourite song of Sam's, which he first heard on a recording of traditional Maori music sung by the famous bass-baritone, Inia te Wiata. For Sam that song captured the Maori emotion he is so fond of, which influenced his decision to move to New Zealand. It seemed to him appropriate that he recognise this in his first important New Zealand rose, hence Matangi became the name that marks the beginning of Sam McGredy's antipodean era and New Zealand's new internationalism.

There are many who feel that Matangi is the best of Sam McGredy's hand-painted roses, but it has not caused Sam to rest on his past glories. If anything, McGredy's New Zealand years have produced his most outstanding roses, with a range of exquisite classics as well as some outstanding innovations of a quality and range to be expected from his huge Portadown operation but hardly from a one-man breeding house in Waitakere City. In the 20 years since his arrival, it has been a performance that could be said to be typical of New Zealand ingenuity and flair, from a man who, in spite of his accent, claims to be a New Zealander. It is a performance that will keep the rose world entranced by the McGredy name for a few decades yet.

In 1980, the painted line continued with Sue Lawley, followed by Maestro in 1981. Very good roses they are, but it was in other areas that the sensations came. In 1980 he produced the miraculous little white Snow Carpet, which proved something to those who were still unsure that roses can do everything in the garden. Snow Carpet was the first compact version of what are now called Procumbent roses, and it is a little ripper, meandering across the ground in every direction, with continuous bursts of tiny white flowers across its shiny, matted foliage.

During the journey that convinced him to emigrate to New Zealand, Sam McGredy is seen here talking to Guide Molly on a visit to Whakarewarewa in 1971. To Sam's right are *(from left to right)* Hette Spek, Niels Poulsen *(sitting)* and Phil Gardner of Avenue Nurseries in Levin.

Prior to this, McGredy had produced the fiercely scarlet Trumpeter, setting his colour performance at the highest standard, and keeping pace with the latest Floribundas. Scarlet appeared too in the searing red of Olympiad, the statuesque Hybrid Tea that was named the official rose of the Los Angeles Olympics. He also made strong claims in the Miniature/Patio field with Eyepaint, Ko's Yellow, Regensberg and Wanaka.

Then, in 1984, came Sexy Rexy, a stunning tender-pink Floribunda that gushes cascades of blooms throughout the season. It is a fantastic rose, one of the greatest ever, with huge sprays of flowers and healthy, disease-resistant, bushy foliage. Not surprisingly it is a multiple award winner, and has been immensely popular. Sexy Rexy became the source of a succession of superb new roses from McGredy, wondrously healthy plants with an abundance that would have seemed incredible just 20 years ago. Kapiti is one, a gorgeous pink groundcover rose; as is the white Patio rose, Whiteout; and the aptly named pink Rexy's Baby. However, it is the full-sized roses that make the best spectacle of the family link, especially Spek's Centennial, Miriam and Auckland Metro, all destined to stake a permanent claim in local gardens. There is also Aotearoa.

For all Sexy Rexy's spectacular arrival and luscious performance, it is the classic form and fragrance of Aotearoa that is the pinnacle of Sam

McGredy's breeding, and a fitting rose to carry the name of the country he has decided he loves. Sam was approached by the New Zealand Government to name a rose for the nation's 150th birthday in 1990, a request Sam considered an honour. He proceeded to select from his latest and brightest seedlings a rose that would not only be a prize winner, but which would become a great favourite with New Zealand's rose growers.

If you were to create a rose to order for New Zealand, a plant that captured the essence of our rose growing history, with blooms that epitomised rose romance here, Aotearoa would be that rose. Sam's choice of this particular plant is both a tribute to his talent, and a delicious piece of rose mystery. He selected the best rose from his seedlings, in itself a process that was sure to bring out something special, for it was the culmination of a quite spectacular career, a career that had made tempting excursions into almost every sphere of rose culture, but which found its mètier in abundance and classic shape. Add to this the McGredy stamp of vigour and health, and you have the perfect style of rose for New Zealand's universal gardener.

As for the rose mystery, simply by attracting McGredy to New Zealand it worked its influence, for none of his talented contemporaries would have suited New Zealand's rose community so well, nor would their roses have complemented its character with such ease. Like Aotearoa, McGredy was made for New Zealand, and in his antipodean roses can be found something of the spirit of this place, a clarity of character as intense and glorious as the new-found wonders of New Zealand wine.

As if to confirm the rose mystery's part, Aotearoa is pink. According to Sam, it is the ideal colour for a gentle people, not knowing when he decided on this special rose that pink is the archetypal New Zealand rose colour, a favourite for at least 170 years. So, pink and perfect, Aotearoa was released in 1990, and quickly became the most popular rose in the country, as easy to grow as it is to fall in love with: a great New Zealand rose, from a great New Zealand breeder.

At Takahanga Marae in Kaikoura roses feature, as they have done in Maori gardens around the country since the first roses appeared at Rangihoua almost 200 years ago.

12 The now rose

Whatever we are now, we were then.
Some days those maps collide
falling into future land.
It seems for hours
we have sat in your car,
almost valentine's day,
I've got a plane to meet and I
hold your rose for you.

for Daphne, *Michael Ondaatje*

For the rose, every season changes. Each year there is a new selection of the breeders' latest efforts on offer, and during the lifetime of this book there will be many springs, many new roses, and many original approaches to rose growing, to rose gardens and to the way we use these seductive flowers and their persuasive imagery.

Roses not only survive, they flourish in modern New Zealand, and as our cultural expression matures, roses are finding a specifically New Zealand voice in the minds and explanations of our artists. Not an entirely new voice, but one that carries the echoes of ancient spiritual ties, a voice that holds both its European past and its Pacific present, its Southern Pacific future. Rose symbolism has adapted to suit every twist of imagination, every change of fashion and social development.

Today, interest in roses has never been greater, carried by a surge of interest in gardening as the baby boomers of the 1950s mellow with the 1990s to fit more comfortably into the soil and growing culture of this country. An image once considered the ultimate in New Zealand kitsch, the chocolate box rose, has gained in sophistication to strengthen its hold on the imagery of our deepest emotions. The rose and its mystery have never had a more expansive presence here, consolidated by the energy and fame of McGredy, the commercial nous of Bell and Schuurman, and the popular inclusion of garden centres and supermarkets.

This presence is not always profound, but as T. S. Elliot observed in his *Burnt Norton* poem, there are many layers of rose imagery, and its origins are deeper than can be gathered from the superficial appearance of roses in our modern world.

High-speed communications have spread western icons, as they have those of other cultural groups, across the globe with a resulting muddle of symbols now circulating via electronics and tourism, including those that have profound meaning as well as those that are extremely banal in their original context. Such symbols may introduce new ideas or foster cross-cultural understanding, but they also run the

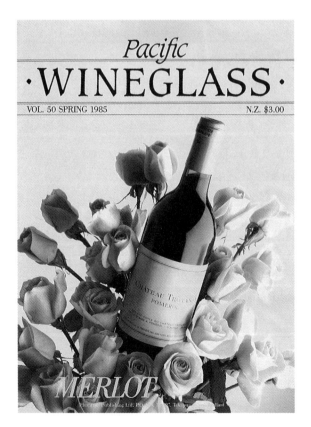

Wine and roses, two of the oldest spiritual symbols of Western civilisation, each representing a half of a sexual whole; rose the female, wine the male.

Aotearoa
Vivian Ward

risk of becoming distorted and losing their original meaning. In every country there are striking examples of this cramming of ideas onto a freeway of interaction. In New Zealand, we now easily accept karioke and sushi, where less than a generation ago we were culturally challenged by wine drinking; in Vietnam, modern brides wear western white and carry roses, symbols of death in their own culture.

The recognisable images of western art are now jostled by those from the Middle East and Asia, but somehow the rose seems to have gained from the clutter. Perhaps this is because the rose mystery has such a complex varied background that it thrives in a global environment. It is strong in both East and West, in high art and in a domestic art culture that has elevated the world of commerce through advertising. In fact, while it is no longer easy to identify what is indigenous, and what is the stuff of a much wider culture that stretches far beyond the range of tentatively bicultural New Zealand, the mongrel past of the rose makes it not only recognisable everywhere but a particularly relevant symbol of our own scrambled lineage.

Rather than dilute our own rose imagery, the incoming symbols here aroused old rose ideas and introduced new ones, as well as confirming many of our own subconscious assumptions. In the last days of 1992 *Time* magazine ran two photographs of the red rose as a symbol of power, one acknowledged for at least 4000 years. In the photographs this ancient sign of power is brandished by two leaders — Serbia's champion of ruthless xenophobia, Slobodan Milosovic, and the embodiment of US democracy, newly elected President, Bill Clinton — who stand at opposite ends of contemporary politics, but for whom the red rose means the same thing: power. Different leaders, different constituents — but the same badge of authority as worn by English King, Henry V when he defeated the French at Agincourt in 1415.

True to its own traditions, commerce prefers to use the sexual implications of roses to sell its products, rather than the rose's claim to power or, worse, its references to transience and death. Advertising is, after all, a 'good news' medium. Sexually implicit red roses are used to flog everything from chocolates to tea and even sex itself, in the form of women's perfume. On television, radio, in newspapers and magazines, the rose's message suits commerce well; we accept it so readily it is a cliché that has not faded, much to the chagrin of rose lovers who would prefer that their passion was not so flagrantly demeaned.

The epitome of commercial power and feminine sexuality as promoted by the world of advertising is undoubtedly the highly priced, glamour perfumes of France, of which the most expensive is 'Joy'. 'Joy' is made predominantly from the finest rose oil, a luxury that was once the exclusive product of the gardens of Provins. Now made in Turkey, Bulgaria and Morocco, where labour is cheap enough to making picking the four tonnes of Kazanlik rose petals needed to produce one kilo of precious oil and still make a profit, rose oil is the high-priced pinnacle of the essential oil business, selling for around NZ$10,000 per kilo. A high enough sum to arouse interest in New Zealand, and 70 years after the farcical attempt to smuggle a Kazanlik cutting out of Bulgaria, rose farming is again being considered as an option for more diverse land-use.

In many ways, the 1990s are a reflection of the 1920s as New Zealand attempts to redefine itself. It is perhaps a measure of increased sophistication that we have not embarked on another piece of industrial espionage to investigate the possibilities of growing roses for otto, or attar of rose, as the luxurious fragrant oil is known. This time the project has been undertaken by government horticultural researchers who secured their Kazanlik, or *R. damascena trigintapetala*, roses from Tasman Bay Roses in Motueka, whose stock originally came from rose breeder and author, Trevor Griffiths. Less dramatic than smuggling them out of Bulgaria, but a more assured way of developing a research block suitable for testing.

The project team began investigations in 1985. Two trial blocks of roses were planted, one by the Department of Scientific and Industrial Research at Riwaka, just outside Motueka, and another by the Ministry of Agriculture and Fisheries at Redbank in Central Otago. After a

The Auckland rose trial garden at Manurewa, framed by native trees.

number of bureaucratic disruptions because of changing government policy, and the end of the Riwaka trial as a result of less than satisfactory results, research continues at Redbank, under Malcolm Douglas of the new New Zealand Institute for Crop and Food Research.

Redbank had its third flower harvest in 1993, picking flowers from the 600 Kazanlik bushes they have growing on their experimental hectare of land. From these, nearly four tonnes of petals were taken and almost one kilogram of high quality rose oil was distilled. It is a successful project so far, proving that very fine oil can be produced from New Zealand-grown roses, but in spite of the extremely high prices gained for this oil, the costs of harvest mean that it is unlikely to become a significant local industry.

New Zealand's rich rose culture does offer other possibilities, however, and with the potential for tourism and for other rose products, as well as small quantities of oil for the local market, there are already a number of people interested in developing some sort of commercial rose farming. Maybe there is a New Zealand perfume with the cachet of 'Joy' somewhere in the future to add a touch of glamour to our own rose mystery, as well as the soaps, pot-pourri and other little pleasures that would come from such a project.

Amidst new opportunities, old industries thrive. In the baby boomers' gardens, roses are flourishing. Garden centres, that hope of the 1960s, have at last come into their own, becoming one of the few commercial sectors to thrive while the country wallowed in the hangover slump that followed the materialist binge of the 1980s. The garden has become a focus of commercial activity as never before, with an avalanche of specialists in magazines, on radio, and on both television networks, a renaissance in garden book publishing, and a new surge of interest in our most popular flower, the rose.

New Zealanders currently buy over 2 million rose plants each year, an amazing statistic that gives monetary substance to the place of roses in this country. All those poetic references to roses, in our literature, art and spiritual make up, can now be seen by accountants in the famous bottom line.

Flourishing garden centres have naturally given an impetus to rose nurseries, especially those of the size and efficiency envisaged by young Laurie Bell over 35 years ago. Bell Roses continues to be the largest rose supplier in the country, and its specialty, Miniatures, has assumed a significant role in the rose trade, with Miniature roses at least as popular now as the full-sized versions. They are roses for now, easy to buy, easy to fit into any living conditions, city flat or rambling country homestead, and they are cheap enough for children to buy as presents for their rose besotted parents, or to start their own rose growing careers. If one were needed, the success of Miniatures is yet another mark of Laurie Bell's remarkable commercial insight, his ability to foresee trends in public attitudes and fashion, a reason for Bell's significant share of the garden rose business.

Frank Schuurman, too, has made a mark with Miniatures, and with the Patio roses that have evolved from these little charmers. Now breeding garden roses as well as cutting plants, Frank grabbed the prestigious RINZ Rose of the Year Award for 1992 with Little Pearl. He also has the prolific yellow, Little Nugget, the delightfully pretty salmon/coral Patio Gem, fragrant Tinkerbell and Little Opal creating a permanent place for him amongst New Zealand rose growers. All are vigorous plants, with perfectly shaped flowers and clear bright colours that show the vitality that has come to be a feature of our roses, and all fit easily into garden landscapes that require more of their roses than tufts of flowers on standard bushes.

Modern gardeners are gradually learning about the virtuosity of garden roses, which is just as well as the new gardeners have more demanding standards for the plants they grow and the things they want them to do. They are guided by the pressures of modern living, especially in urban areas, and by the enormous range of information available on gardening in numerous gardening magazines and books, of which roses always claim a significant proportion. It is almost 160 years since Mrs. Gore's famous rose book was first published, and her efforts have been followed by an immense range of English language publications that address the garden rose, its cultivation, history and landscaping potential. Gardening book specialists, Touchwood Books, regularly list many more rose titles in their catalogues than they do any other single plant species, often amounting to over 120 current and second-hand examples of particular rose views and ideas.

This flood has made increasingly literate gardeners better informed, and encouraged them to extend the range of their gardening expectations. For over 30 years roses have needed to be healthy, vigorous and floriferous to attract support, but they must now also be adaptable to a wide variety of landscaping demands, offering ground cover, portability, border appeal and height, as well as abundance and rich floral display. Books and articles tell gardeners what can be done, and they go to garden centres intent on buying what they need to transform those ideas into reality.

Breeders have performed well in meeting these changes, and there is now a rose for almost every plan, every potential landscape. To make sales, however, rose sellers must present their plants so that they catch the eye of browsers in garden centres, and they must market what they have in the way any commodity is marketed, with slick advertising and publicity. The new world is a place where the consumer is in control; informed, demanding, and fickle, but with more money to indulge their latest fad than ever before. Distribution and packaging for this market is a long way from the moss and dung solutions that Lippiatt's used on their mail-order roses 60 years ago. Roses are now delivered in containers from the nursery to every centre from Invercargill to Kaitaia, and they must arrive healthy to look as good in the garden centre as they will in the garden, or they will not sell.

It is a hard environment, one that has added rapid change and the quirks of fashion to the once conservative commerce of plant nurseries. Changes that have driven a number of famous old names from the rose nursery field, and nurtured the development of new companies more adept at meeting the challenge companies like Egmont Roses, who are able to match nursery professionalism with marketing skill.

Egmont Roses founder, John Martin, came to New Zealand in 1971 from a job managing a rose nursery in England. He joined the established Taranaki firm of Duncan and Davies, for whom he grew roses on a contract basis until he started a nursery on his own behalf, working part time, in 1979. Since that first crop of 3000 plants, John has gradually taken over the rose business as his old company vacated it, and has subsequently built Egmont Roses into one of the largest nurseries in the country, producing some 350,000 plants for sale through garden centres and other outlets nationwide. Simultaneously Egmont has established a reputation for healthy roses, and has attracted the agency rights for a number of substantial international breeders, notably Poulsen, Bear Creek, Dot, Warner, Ilsink and McGredy, for whom Egmont is the home nursery.

John Martin has also started in earnest on the long fraught road to establishing himself as a breeder, a step that promises to extend the McGredy dynamism in another New Zealand direction. The momentum of generations of rose tradition, our own special climate and soils, and an enthusiastic practicality that is a feature of our attitude to excellence, is a sound basis for a healthy future for local breeders. McGredy has led the charge, and while the great man has retired, his last efforts will continue to appear on the market through most of the 1990s. Frank Schuurman and John Martin are the next generation of New Zealand breeders, and both have the professional edge, as well as the enthusiasm, that is likely to ensure that the name of New Zealand continues to be respected amongst the world's rose growers.

Certainly the basics are there for a flourishing international reputation. The growing conditions are perfect, and there is enough legal and social recognition of the creative role of the breeder. Coupled with the buoyancy of the industry, there is no reason not to expect continued success, especially if the Rose Introducers of New Zealand organisation continues to encourage and promote breeders' work.

Back in the early 1970s, Sam McGredy knew that the newly introduced Breeders' Rights legislation would not be enough by itself to ensure that breeders were paid their royalties, nor that their roses would be adequately promoted without some form of co-ordinated support within the nursery industry. After much lobbying, he persuaded the leading rose growers and breeders' agents to form such a body; the first meeting of Rose Introducers of New Zealand, RINZ, was held at Auckland International Airport in 1974. Since then it has served in just the way Sam hoped, by promoting the concept of breeders to the whole rose community, promoting roses, and by establishing a process by which royalties can be collected and passed on. Forming RINZ also greatly improved the level of co-operation amongst rose nurseries, and built a sense of unity that is essential if the best interests of the rose as a garden plant are to be promoted.

The issue of royalties has forced RINZ to be professional, for it requires meticulous attention to detail and a high standard of accounting to maintain the necessary accuracy. Each new rose is introduced by its agent only after careful consideration of its potential appeal to New Zealand gardeners, because RINZ charges agents $180 a year, per variety, as a registration fee. For this, each plant sold returns a maximum of 99 cents per bush or standard and 50 cents per Miniature in royalties to the breeder or their agent, depending on how long the plant has been on the market, with new and popular roses bringing in the highest return per plant. RINZ takes 5 per cent of the royalties for administration and conducting random audits of the 44 rose growers around the country, to make sure that their royalty returns are honest. Of the remainder, the normal agency agreement sees 50 per cent go to the breeder, and 50 per cent retained by the agent.

In mid 1993 there were 257 protected rose varieties in New Zealand, and the turnover in royalties had grown from $116,000 in 1974 to $415,000 in 1991. This is not a huge profit for breeders, but it is significant, and is substantially more than it was before RINZ was established. While New Zealand supports a comparatively successful rose growing industry, with an estimated annual worth of some $30 million for both garden and cut flower sections of the business, it takes large sales to repay an agent for the cost of registering breeding rights (approximately 3500 bush roses, or 7000 Miniatures, usually taking a number of years). The large international rose markets are where the real profits of rose breeding are to be found, and it is there that the New Zealand rose breeders who are set to follow Sam McGredy must be active if the efforts of Sam and his fellow RINZ members are to be consolidated. The selection of McGredy's Olympiad as the official rose for the 1984 Los Angeles Olympics is the sort of success that turns fame into dollars, with huge numbers in the United States buying this big, red rose.

The most public activity of RINZ has been the establishment of a rose trial ground at the Auckland Regional Botanic Gardens, in Manurewa, South Auckland. Since 1990, new roses have been trialled in mass-planted beds in an exquisitely lush rose garden, over a period of three years, for their suitability to Auckland growing conditions. Each November the best Hybrid Tea, best Floribunda/shrub, best Climber, best Miniature, best fragrance, and overall Auckland Rose of the Year are judged. What is unique about these awards is that they are made by popular vote of invited guests, mostly rose enthusiasts, rather than professional judges or growers, a sign of today's focus on the rose in the garden rather than the bloom on the judging bench.

As bright and fashionable as the new world of roses is, it is not just new roses that are finding favour with gardeners. It may be a sign that as New Zealand matures it is discovering the richness of its own history, it may be that the romance of roses arouses dreams of an imagined past when life was simpler and more pleasant. Certainly the idyllic country cottage awash with roses is an idea that has moved gardeners in the past to look for plants and landscapes that give the idea life, so it is not surprising that the recent flush of glamorous, practical, modern roses has been matched by a surge of interest in 'old-fashioned' roses, whose appeal is touched by the tenderness of memory, its suggestion of loss and sweetness a perfect example of the rose paradox.

In the context of roses, old-fashioned seems to mean roses from a remembered childhood and the gardens of grandparents, of mellow memories of summers with no rain, of roses with wonderful fragrance. Old-fashioned roses are romantic territory, romance that often glosses over the realities of disease, shy-flowering and straggly, ugly plants, factors that saw such plants replaced by those that flourished and flowered with ease. Certainly the pleasures of many older roses were brief and isolated, and modern varieties like Aotearoa, with its wickedly seductive perfume, sensual pink blooms and abundance, are more than a match for many a pretty thing at the end of a rod of hard thorns.

Many older roses, however, suffered for no other reason than they became unfashionable, and the current enthusiasm for old roses has given gardeners a chance to revisit some of these charming varieties and discover the characteristics that once made them popular. Roses like Albertine and Bloomfield Abundance, or Cécile Brunner, are a wonderful addition to any modern garden, as are many of the species roses. Even that old hedge plant, Sweet Briar, banned as it is by bureaucracy, gives a fragrant edge to any garden with its gentle whiff of apple on the summer wind.

Nancy Steen was the old rose champion who brought the value of these beauties back into view. Based in Auckland, she not only used a stunning range of roses in her own garden, but she travelled the country seeking out, identifying and often salvaging roses from the roadside, from old gardens, churchyards and derelict farms. Her book, *The Charm of Old Roses*, first published in 1966 and again in 1987, has become a rose classic, packed as it is with enthusiasm and anecdote, and a comfortable stroll through New Zealand's rose world that is far more expansive than a trip to the municipal rose gardens or the local garden centre.

A measure of Nancy Steen's influence is the garden of old-fashioned and species roses that has been developed alongside the Parnell Rose Gardens in Auckland, named after Nancy and visited each year by thousands of budding rose enthusiasts. It is a living glimpse of our rose past that breaks the New Zealand tradition of dead museums and preserved buildings, one that grows and changes with the seasons, creating a link with our rich gardening history, as well as providing inspiration for present and future gardeners.

Another mark of the interest in old-fashioned roses is the gardening club known as Heritage Roses New Zealand. Initiated by amateur historian Ken Nobbs and rose enthusiast Toni Sylvester, it was established in 1980, with the first *Heritage Rose Journal* published in August of that year. In it, Ken Nobbs wrote of Sweet Briar growing at Oihi, near the original mission station established by Samuel Marsden alongside Ruatara's pa, and also of the species roses, *R. banksia* and *R. laevigata*, both of which have grown in New Zealand since at least the 1850s.

Heritage Roses New Zealand continues to flourish, with members throughout the country, garden visits and quarterly issues of their chatty journal keeping gardeners informed about 'new' old roses, historical details about rose growing in New Zealand and abroad, book reviews, and other details of interest to those who garden with an eye on the past. Like the various rose societies, it also serves to promote interest in our rose history, and the growing of roses with a tradition.

This journey through New Zealand's rose history began its local portion in the hands of the great Ngapuhi innovator, Ruatara, and it seems appropriate, indeed even a logical extension of the rose mystery, that this book should again finish in the hands of the Maori, and again on the site of another cultural confluence of great significance. Since Ruatara there has been no special Maori feature of roses in this country, other than as a symbol of the assimilation of flower gardening into Maori culture, and so there have been no Maori rose traditions separate from those of Pakeha New Zealanders. In this guise, roses are to be found on marae and in Maori gardens around the country, much as they are found in Pakeha gardens.

At Kaikoura, on the east coast of the South Island, however, roses are part of a dramatic work of art. The Ngati Kuri, part of Ngai Tahu, have reclaimed an important piece of their ancestral land at Kaikoura, an ancient pa site that watches over the impressive sweep of mountain-dominated coast below. On it they have built a marae, Takahanga, a place that stands as a symbol of their Maori heritage, their Maori-Pakeha history, and their vitality. It is as powerful a piece of New Zealand art as any that has ever been done, with a voice and a vision that includes the land, history, traditions, and the different cultures that have influenced its making. The decoration of the whare nui, 'Maru Kaitatea', is stunning in its boldness: contemporary Pakeha artists have been allowed their place, and gardens, for food and decoration, are a feature. Entry to Takahanga is through what was once the historic gate-way to the original marae at the centre of the old pa, and the fence that leads to this new gate is lined with roses. If Takahanga is a glimpse of the future in this country, if our culture is to grow together and our history is to be celebrated, there could be no more significant symbol of our growing past.

Illustrations list